A HANDBOOK

FOR THE STUDY OF

BOOK HISTORY

IN THE UNITED STATES

A HANDBOOK

FOR

THE STUDY OF

BOOK HISTORY

IN THE

UNITED STATES

Ronald J. Zboray

and

Mary Saracino Zboray

CENTER FOR THE BOOK · LIBRARY OF CONGRESS

WASHINGTON, D.C.

© 2000 by Ronald J. Zboray and Mary Saracino Zboray

LIBRARY OF CONGRESS CATALOGING-IN-PUBLICATION DATA

Zboray, Ronald J.
 A handbook for the study of book history in the United States / Ronald J.
Zboray and Mary Saracino Zboray.
  p. cm.
 Includes bibliographical references and index.
 ISBN 0-8444-1015-2 (alk. paper)
  1. Books–History–Study and teaching–United States.
 2. Books–History–Research–United States. 3. Books–History–Bibliography.
 I. Zboray, Mary Saracino, 1953– II. Center for the Book. III. Title.

Z4.35.U6 Z36 2000
002'.071'073–dc21   00-029456

Contents

Preface

ENCOURAGING the study of books is a principal aim of the Center for the Book in the Library of Congress. The center was created as a public-private partnership by Congress in 1977 to stimulate public interest in books, reading, and the printed word. In pursuit of this goal, the center sponsors a varied program of projects of interest to scholars and the general public.

The scholarly side of the center's activities includes lectures, conferences, publications, and joint projects with other institutions and with the Library of Congress's subject divisions. The center's major contributions to the increasingly popular field of book history include the Engelhard Lectures on the Book, cosponsored with the Library's Rare Book and Special Collections Division, and books resulting from symposia, such as *Literacy in Historical Perspective* (1983), *Getting the Books Out: Papers of the Chicago Conference on the Book in Nineteenth-Century America* (1987), *Publishing and Readership in Revolutionary France and America* (1993), and *The Book in the Islamic World* (1995). In addition, Alice D. Schreyer's *History of Books: A Guide to Selected Resources at the Library of Congress* (1987) is a pioneering introduction to one institution's resources for the study of the history of the book and allied fields.

The preparation of this handbook was suggested by Librarian of Congress James H. Billington to Jonathan Rose and myself at a conference, "Libraries and Reading in Times of Cultural Change," held in Vologda, Russia, in June 1996. Rose, who was then president of the Society for the History of Authorship, Reading, and Publishing (SHARP), immediately thought of Ronald and Mary Zboray as potential authors.

The result is this compact, clearly written introduction to the subject and literature of book history. The importance of the field, according to the Zborays, resides in "a simple fact: in the history of the United States as a nation, books and other print materials are the most prevalent and articulate cultural artifacts." This handbook is an insightful overview and survey which will stimulate further interest in books, reading, and the printed word.

The Center for the Book is grateful to Ronald and Mary Zboray for this thoughtful contribution to book history and print culture studies. Its publication is made possible by a financial contribution to the Center for the Book by its founder, historian Daniel J. Boorstin, who served as Librarian of Congress from 1975 to 1987. The Daniel J. and Ruth F. Boorstin Fund, established when Dr. Boorstin retired in 1987, supports several key Center for the Book activities. Thanks to the Boorstins, we are able to share the work of Ronald and Mary Zboray with a wide audience.

The Center for the Book is a catalyst in the world of books and print culture. It operates primarily through partnerships with affiliated state centers, national educational and civic groups, and academic and research organizations. Since 1977, the center has published more than forty books and fifty pamphlets. Information about the Center for the Book and its programs, publications, and partnership networks can be found on the center's web site: <http://www.loc.gov/loc/cfbook>.

John Y. Cole
Director
Center for the Book

Acknowledgments

WERE WE to thank all the many people who have helped us with our research into the history of the book over the years, the list would probably be as long as this entire handbook. We must confine the expression of our gratitude here to the select few who have furthered the completion of this handbook. Chief among those are John Y. Cole, of the Library of Congress's Center for the Book, and Jonathan Rose, former president of the Society for the History of Authorship, Reading, and Publishing, both of whom provided sage advice and welcome encouragement. Tom Knoles at the American Antiquarian Society kindly gave us his time to explain varieties of publishers' manuscript records in the collections, and Jane Pomeroy, in discussions with us, drew upon her vast knowledge of early nineteenth-century engraving and illustration. A portion of the book was written in New England during a fall 1997 research leave generously granted by the Georgia State University Department of History and funded by a Research Initiation Grant from that university. Discussions with our GSU colleague Brian Armstrong helped clarify for us the mysteries of descriptive bibliography. Not to be forgotten among those to whom we owe our deepest thanks are the many dedicated scholars whose work is cited in these pages, who have contributed—and many of whom still contribute—to the field of the history of the book in the United States and elsewhere.

Rockport, Mass., January 1999

A HANDBOOK

FOR THE STUDY OF

BOOK HISTORY

IN THE UNITED STATES

I. Introduction

ON A Tuesday evening in 1858, Christopher Keith, an unemployed platmaker in Providence, Rhode Island, wrote in his diary about a cherished piece of printed matter:

> I have been reading the Dial published some few years ago by the transcendentalists. It is beautifully written and contains some very fine literary pieces. It was a good publication in its day but did not have a long life. It was edited by Emerson and a few others of the same stamp. It is a very good volume to read now although it has attained some considerable age. But that is the case usually with works of real merit; they are like wine—they improve by age. So may I I [*sic*] grow wiser and better as life wears away.

Having found or perhaps borrowed a worn copy of the *Dial* that was probably nearly twenty years old, Keith discovered he could still enjoy the "beautiful" writing and literary quality, but he also mourned the aging of the once fresh and avant-garde periodical. He furthermore compared it with himself, a living human being who, like the *Dial,* was also growing older. "So may I grow wiser and better," he hoped, and "improve by age." To Keith's mind, printed materials are like people: they are born and they age—preferably for the better—and they eventually wear away.[1]

Keith's observations about books are wise ones, for books are indeed like people in that they are created, they have a life span in which they move about and change physically, and they grow old. Books, however, have the advantage of an existence that often stretches over centuries, for we still can find some books that were born of the first printing presses of the fifteenth century. Although many books live longer than people, book history is like human history—or biography—in that it is possible to study a book's life span. We can learn about how it came into being: who authored it, and how it was printed, sewn together, bound, and published. We can ask where it traveled through life, how it passed through the hands of peddlers or the racks of bookstores and into the collections of libraries or private owners. We can then find out how a book became part of people's lives when they brought it into their homes to read, letting it "speak" to them as they read it, enjoying its company, disagreeing with it sometimes, completely misunderstanding it at others, remembering a few of its most vibrant characteristics, and, perhaps, learning something new from it.

We can always learn something new from books. They prevent us from becoming solipsistic or preoccupied and limited by our own peculiar way of seeing the world. Harriet Low, an American living in China in 1831, said it well when she wrote in her diary, "What should I do it if it were not for books? I am sure I should get quite sick of my own company."[2] It still rings true today. Books remind us that we are not the center of the world, but they also assure us that we are not alone. When we read a book written by someone else, we listen to that person's thoughts, compare them to our own, and ponder them. But we do not only have to read a book to share its company. We can also look at its illustrations, its bindings, its paper, or its print, and in these we can discover something new as well: how the book was produced. When we walk into a library to borrow books or into a bookstore to buy them, we find out something new, too: about how books are disseminated or made available for us to borrow or own.

This handbook offers one way of learning something new from books by understanding their production, dissemination, and, finally, consumption, through our reading of them. Anyone who is interested in learning more about the history of printed matter can become a historian of books by applying some tried-and-true methodologies or even inventing a new approach. It does not necessarily take specialized knowledge to study books. People from various fields—communications, education, history, journalism, library science, and literature—all share an interest in book history. In fact, book history is sometimes called "print culture," to emphasize its scope, which includes all printed matter and the world that surrounds it. Individuals such as collectors, booksellers, and independent scholars are also involved with the history of books.[3] What is most intriguing about the field is its all-encompassing nature, which draws together people with diverse interests and accomplishments.

This handbook will present various methodologies for studying book history. In a small space, it attempts to provide breadth of scope by weighing, comparing, and contrasting the various approaches to book history, primarily in the United States. Although the field of book history has global dimensions, this handbook is chiefly concerned with the study of books produced in this country. It also points out standard sources that can be used as starting points for discovering one's own path through book history. Readers may develop their own methodologies and use materials within easy reach: book and magazine collections, materials from local public libraries or historical societies, even old letters in the attic. A home computer with access to web pages and on-line library catalogs may prove useful as well, but mainly as a research tool, for this handbook is not aimed at the study of electronic texts. Although the "no longer so new" technology of the Internet may seem to be replacing texts made of ink and paper, many observers expect that "the book will be with us for many centuries to come."[4] Despite widespread reliance upon computers for information today, most of human history has been intertwined with the history of printed materials, and this handbook addresses that history.

A. WHY IS BOOK HISTORY IMPORTANT?

Book history owes its significance to a simple fact: in the history of the United States as a nation, books and other print materials are the most prevalent and articulate cultural artifacts. Paintings, music, architecture, or other cultural expressions can be evocative, but they do not "speak" as directly as print does. Manuscript materials, especially letters and diaries, of course, are articulate (and offer insights that printed materials cannot), but for the most part they have a limited circulation. Print is much more a collective product, and it addresses a public. Insofar as print crosses regions, demographic categories, ethnicities, races, genders, and occupations, it can offer insights into the life of Americans as a people.

The study of print thus offers a wide-angle view of American civilization. Print touches upon nearly every one of the many specialized areas of human endeavor in our society. Whether among scientists or race-car aficionados, much information exchange occurs through print. And because print is a more or less permanent record, it provides, in the words of John Y. Cole, a "storehouse" from which future generations may draw.[5] In public and private libraries across the country, readers may go to this storehouse and draw from it. Researchers can move quickly through various bodies of knowledge and expression to obtain pictures of infinite detail or of bird's-eye generalization.

B. WHAT IS THE FIELD ABOUT?

The several disciplines that touch book history all share an understanding: printed artifacts do not give direct insight into the past; rather, that insight is *mediated*. That is to say, meaning does not leap directly from writers' to readers' minds through printed pages, but rather is produced through interventions, or mediations. For example, a writer writes for a "market"; editors and publishers shape and reconfigure the writer's work into book form and decide upon its packaging and distribution; booksellers display the book where potential buyers may be likely to see it; finally, different readers understand the book in a variety of ways. By the time the book is read, it has traveled through many such mediations. Some scholars see these mediations as distortions—just as messages become mangled when whispered from person to person in a line—but book historians take these mediations as their principal object of study. Why? Because the mediations of producers, disseminators, and consumers of printed materials provide insight into how a society produces meaning.

C. OVERVIEW AND HISTORY OF THE FIELD

The study of printed books is nearly as old as printing itself, which in the Western world dates to the fifteenth century. Today's book history, however, originated in a nineteenth-century intellectual practice called "historicism." Historicism had exhorted researchers to pile up details about the past until a picture emerged that expressed a *zeitgeist,* or spirit of the age. Such researchers sought to know as much as possible about authors and their books before venturing interpretations of what was written on the page. They used this knowledge to evaluate works and understand them.

Modernist critics in the early twentieth century attacked this literary historicism. They argued that interpretation can begin without a mountain of biographical and bibliographical detail. Believe the tale (the "text"), they held, not the teller, and certainly not the teller's publisher. Rather than inquire about authorship, publishing, or reading, these critics read texts closely to understand form and structure. Biography and bibliography thus became marginalized.

The history of the book is not simply a return to the earlier tradition, however, but part of a "new historicism." What makes it new is that it rejects the notion of a *zeitgeist* common to nearly all participants in a culture.[6] New historicists tend to see culture as a field of contests, contradictions, and interests rooted in specific conditions. For book historians, this means that people must navigate among conflicting authorities expressed through print; in some cases, readers may use print to "fashion" themselves, their very identities.[7] The rich diversity of print materials thus does not challenge book historians to devise an all-encompassing cultural interpretation that reduces historical experience to overly simple structures.[8] Rather, these historians find the details of the production, dissemination, and reception of a printed text to be important in and of themselves.

We can best understand the development of American book history as a transition from the old to the new historicism. This occurred in four consecutive, overlapping phases: antiquarian, consensus, neo-consensus, and new historicist.

The antiquarian phase, which dates at least to Isaiah Thomas's *History of Printing in America* (1810), saw the accumulation of information about printers and their imprints. The phase culminates in the work of Douglas C. McMurtrie, who not only compiled state imprints with Works Progress Administration (WPA) funding in the 1930s, but also popularized the topic through radio appearances. He, along with Hellmut Lehmann-Haupt, Ruth Shepard Graniss, Lawrence Wroth, and others, forged the welter of facts into a narrative of the development of production and dissemination of American books. It was a story aimed at collectors, rare-book librarians and dealers, bibliographers, and people interested in Americana.

The consensus phase emerged during World War II. As many U.S. historians embraced intellectual history, arguing that Americans had always agreed on issues that mattered, some book historians lent support to this view. Two examples of this phase are James D. Hart and Frank Luther Mott, who in the late 1940s plumbed the nature of American reading taste. William Charvat went the furthest among this group: he struggled to find a rationale for an independent history of publishing, but ultimately gave up, as he realized in 1959 that publishing history was "relevant to literary history only in so far as it can be shown to be, ultimately, a shaping influence on literature."[9] It would be left to John Tebbel in the 1970s to write the monumental culmination of the first two phases of book history. The audience for such works was broad, but mostly focused in academe.

By the time Tebbel published the final volume of his history in 1981, the neo-consensus phase had emerged. Researchers in this phase reacted to a movement called the new social history, which celebrated diversity, local history, and the use of quantitative methods, and downplayed the formal printed discourse that had absorbed consensus historians. Using largely qualitative methods, neo-consensus book historians stressed cultural unification through print, the role of the Protestant vernacular as a dominant cultural force, and the convergence of high and low culture on a consensual middle ground.[10] They placed little emphasis on issues of race, class, and gender.

This phase emerged in the shadow of significant developments in the history of the book in Western Europe. Two of the most influential figures were Americans. One was Robert Darnton, who introduced the field to many American academics; his *Business of Enlightenment,* published in 1979, was an artful demonstration of the practices of the *histoire du livre* school in France. The other was Elizabeth Eisenstein, whose book, *The Printing Press as an Agent of Change,* appeared in the same year as Darnton's and picked up on themes popularized in the 1960s by Marshall McLuhan, though with a lucidity never reached by him. But these American developments paled before those in France, especially as seen in the four-volume *Histoire de l'édition française* (1983–86). By the end of the decade several similar multi-volume collaborative histories of the book were in the works, including an American project at the American Antiquarian Society, under the general editorship of David D. Hall, and a British project emerging from Donald F. McKenzie in the Book Trade History Group (both of these were inaugurated in 1988). Although these massive works are aimed at a wide audience, the neo-consensus scholarship has so far mostly appeared as monographs for specialists or as articles in limited-circulation scholarly journals.

The most recent phase of the field of American book history, the new historicist, grew out of the institutional base of the neo-consensus phase and even shared with it conference platforms and volumes of essays. In its early stages, the phase could be recognized by a reluctance to react against the new social history and a corresponding willingness to incorporate it. This meant that book historians were now paying attention to issues of gender, class, and, to a lesser degree, race. This development can be seen in Cathy N. Davidson's *Revolution and Word* (1986), which heralded the arrival of the new historicist phase. Scholars such as Richard D. Brown and William Gilmore were unwilling to make the types of generalizations about national culture seen among neo-consensus researchers and instead tended to ponder the experience of individuals, often of common origins, within the local and historically specific contexts of their lives. The overall emphasis of new historicist scholarship has been more on reading than publishing, so it has attracted an academic audience drawn from communications, cultural studies, literature, and social and cultural history.

Although each phase (since the antiquarian one) developed out of its predecessor, not all book history researchers have participated in these changes. Insofar as the four phases currently coexist, they generally enrich one another with the peculiar strengths of their respective viewpoints.

D. WHAT QUESTIONS DO BOOK HISTORIANS DEBATE?

Among the important questions book historians debate are the following:

- Did a reading revolution take place in America, from a period in which few books were read intensively to one in which many books were read once and quickly? If such a revolution occurred, when did it happen, and who was affected by it?

- To what extent do texts contain clues about how (and by whom) they were read? Do printed texts virtually dictate the way they are received by readers?

- To what extent did reading help people of an earlier day individualize? Did it also serve a social purpose, by bonding friends, families, and communities?

- How much did a centralized print culture contribute to the forging of an American national identity?

- At what point did American publishing change from a so-called gentleman's trade to a big business?

- When did the profession of authorship emerge in the United States, and how have conditions of authorship affected the creation of a uniquely American literature?

- How autonomous have authors been in dealing with publishers?

- Do authors have solid idea about the nature of their audiences?

- Are publishers creators of taste or servants of it? Or are they servants of larger power interests in society?

- Does the economics of publishing for the widest market silence minority voices and further reproduce the viewpoint of the many?

E. HOW CAN PEOPLE PARTICIPATE IN BOOK HISTORY?

There are many ways for people to take part in book history. Fundamentally, of course, anyone who picks up a book to read, either on his or her own or through book club selections or class assignments, becomes part of book history to some extent, especially if the encounter leads to questions about the mediations that went into producing the book, such as who wrote it or where it came from. If the book is not recently published (or written), such pondering even more resembles what historians of the book do. However, the field of book history amounts to more than simply appreciating and reading old books and wondering about them: it offers more systematic inquiry into the mediations that printed materials have gone through between conception and reception (reading is only one type of reception). By pursuing such systematic inquiry, a wide variety of people of all ages can enhance their understanding of what a book means within the flow of history.

There are many ways for people to take part in book history. Parents and teachers can introduce children to books for young readers produced in different times. They can then ask "discovery" questions, prompting children to compare the look of the books, the types of illustrations, and so forth. Field trips to historic museums with print shops can provide enjoyable educational opportunities. Even computers can be placed at the service of book history for children: for example, after introducing children to several types of frontier newspapers, parents or teachers can have them try to design a newspaper of their own with appropriate typography and organization.

Students in high school or college can add a book history dimension to term papers and other research projects. For example, a report on a famous author might include some consideration of the publisher (what other books did the house publish at about that time? did this author stay with one publisher or work with several at different times?). If any first editions of the author's works are available, some bibliographical description of them could be part of the report.

For people of all ages (though mostly for adults) there is a "community of the book"—a network of organizations devoted in one way or another to promoting the book in America. Most of these organizations hold public meetings, and many have volunteer opportunities. The Library of Congress sponsors state and local Centers for the Book, and these centers, in turn, lend their support to a wide range of public activities (for details, see the Center for the Book's web site at http://www.loc.gov/loc/cfbook). There are innumerable regional and local rare and antiquarian book fairs and similar events, where people can browse through old newspapers, pamphlets, and books—and perhaps purchase one to make book history a part of their own life.

For people who want to learn even more about book history, there is the "community of the book" on the Internet. For example, by visiting the web site of the Society for the History of Authorship, Reading, and Publishing (SHARP) at <http://www.indiana.edu/~sharp>, one can retrospectively "listen" to on-line conversations of book history scholars since 1992.

Another way to become involved is through specialized courses of study. Most graduate schools of library science offer courses in book history or one of its subfields as part of their professional education. At the undergraduate level, courses related to book history are offered by departments of communications, English, and journalism. Qualified graduate students can take part in some summer programs, like those at the University of Virginia and the American Antiquarian Society. Finally, there is a vast journal literature related to book history (see the appendix). There, it is possible to follow topics in depth and encounter the various approaches employed by book historians—as well as scouting opportunities for publishing one's own work in book history.

In what follows, we discuss specific ideas for study in book history and related projects, and we note some areas in which little work has been done. But it is easy to see that book history holds some relevance for just about everyone and that everyone—from the toddler to the scholar—can find some way to participate in this exciting field. We also discuss sources for book history and consider some methods of using them. We hope to convey the range and richness available to people wanting to become involved with book history at all levels of expertise.

II. How to Locate and Use Sources

A. WHERE TO BEGIN

Essential sources for the history of the book are surprisingly abundant and easily accessible, yet they are little used, except by librarians and other specialists. Part of what libraries do is to help people find out where to look for information. The set of directions is usually given as a library call number, along with a description of the book or periodical. The description usually includes the author's name, title, place and date of publication, and publisher's name (or title of the periodical). These are the most basic elements of *bibliography,* or the descriptive study of books.

Bibliography as a field of study long ago moved beyond these simple elements to include very complex descriptions, but they still usually serve to identify a specific publication. This information can be combined and sorted in various ways. For example, a chronological list of an author's published works may suggest the rough outlines of his or her career. The number of works published in different cities can be compared, as a way to track the publishing industry. Titles can be analyzed for the prevalence of certain words or phrases. Above all, basic bibliographical information can hint at the number of different books written by a particular author, dealing with a certain subject, produced by a certain publisher, or published in a specific place or year.

Some of this information is difficult to assemble because most catalogs are organized by author and title; still, two other points of access do often appear: subjects and standard library call numbers. Because subject indexing practices vary over time and between indexers, standard library classifications, such as Dewey decimal and Library of Congress, are a surer guide to locating groups of related works. For example, the "Z" class in the Library of Congress system includes volumes related to the history of books and other aspects of bibliography.

Much of what has been said so far will be familiar to people who use libraries frequently, but that is why the history of books is something almost everyone can appreciate and to which they can contribute. We can build upon what we already know in order to understand better the place and meaning of books in the past.

I. GENERAL SOURCES

Undoubtedly the single most important resource for the study of the history of the book in the United States is the Library of Congress's *National Union Catalog* (*NUC*). Its 685 volumes represent the book, pamphlet, map, atlas, and music holdings in the Library of Congress (some periodicals have been catalogued as well), along with items from other major libraries. The *NUC* is thus a fair representation of just about every standard American publication—and many foreign ones, too—issued before 1956. And it is available in most urban public and university libraries. Each *NUC* entry looks like a photoduplication of a printed or typed library card. From a quick glance at *NUC,* the researcher can get an overview of the history of a popular book's various editions or the range of books an author may have written.

The *NUC*'s searching limitations can be overcome somewhat by using the various electronic catalogs of the Library of Congress itself or, especially, those of some contributing libraries, such as the Harvard University library.[11] Coverage in these catalogs is good for the period since 1955, where *NUC* leaves off. Of course, all electronic catalogs still need to be approached with caution, because usually not all items appearing in conventional library card catalogs or printed dictionaries are represented by corresponding electronic records—although at some future date they may well be. Access to these electronic catalogs requires only a computer with a modem or Internet connection; through these information can be downloaded for further processing.[12]

a. Bibliographies

The indispensable starting point for American book history is G. Thomas Tanselle's *Guide to the Study of United States Imprints* (1971). Nothing else compares with it in breadth and depth of coverage on publishing. Although its treatment of authors and booksellers is not very comprehensive (and it considers readers only implicitly), it is organized by useful topics. For the period after 1971, there is no single source that brings together research on various phases of the history of the book. One notable exception is the *Annual Bibliography of the History of the Printed Book and Libraries* (published in the Netherlands by various houses), which has provided good international coverage since 1970. Beyond this, the best access to secondary sources is through the various specialized journals listed in the appendix at the end of this book.

b. Imprint Lists

Lists of imprints differ from the library catalogs discussed above in that they do not represent books found in specific collections, but rather list everything known to have been printed in a certain place, usually within a range of time. This information is assembled, through arduous labor, from a variety of sources. These imprint lists range from ones that focus on particular states to those treating nations or regions.

For years, researchers in early American history have relied upon a trio of such lists by Charles Evans (to 1800), Ralph Shaw and Richard H. Shoemaker (continuing until 1819), and Shoemaker alone (through 1829), but these lists are not comprehensive. The American Antiquarian Society's North American Imprints Program (NAIP) has attempted to fill in the gaps with an on-line catalog that gives perhaps the most in-depth bibliographical description ever afforded such a vast array of imprints.[13] This on-line resource also permits unusually detailed queries, down to the names of publishers, printers, or booksellers that may appear on the title page, and it allows for combinations of different types of searches.

Both the paper and on-line versions of these early American imprint lists have their counterparts in a microform collection produced by Readex Corporation, which contains nearly all titles published in the colonies and nation to 1820. University research libraries across the country hold this invaluable research tool, making it accessible to most Americans. Because the items are photographically reproduced, it is possible to study these images typographically for page formatting or for various printer's marks.

Nothing compares with this source for the later period, for a good reason: beginning in the 1830s, the publishing industry in the United States expanded dramatically. In addition to using *NUC* and electronic catalogs, researchers must turn to the industry's own compendiums of standard trade publications, which were produced to facilitate business—past equivalents of today's *Books in Print*. These sources are most valuable for understanding the nature of the annual output of the American publishing industry. They provide the type of chronological access and pricing information that general sources generally do not.

c. Trade Papers

The annual publishing trade lists provide a systematic overview of output, but another rich source brings researchers into the nitty-gritty of the industry itself—trade papers. These emerged with the industrialization of publishing just before the Civil War. These papers, then as now, are filled with gossip, tidbits of information on a wide variety of publications, editorial pieces pondering trade issues, profiles of specific houses, and, perhaps most important, discussions of such issues as the relative merits of advertising techniques, the reasons why certain books sold while others did not, and advice about the ever shifting nature of the reading public.[14]

d. Trade Directories

Trade directories facilitate communication within the industry by providing information about firms and personnel. *American Booktrade Directory* (originally titled *American Book Trade Manual*) has been the standard source since 1915, but local counterparts have appeared throughout the twentieth century. For example, the *Printing Trades Blue Book* has appeared in a New York metropolitan edition since 1916.

Directories of this sort dwindle as we move back into the nineteenth century, however, and become more frequent again only for mid-century and before. These earlier directories differ from later ones in that they were assembled by scholars from a variety of sources as a service to bibliographical specialists and rare-book collectors. Such works usually focus on specific cities in particular periods.

These directories offer rich opportunities for research in the history of the book, yet so far few researchers have taken advantage of them. The information appearing in these directories can be entered into a computer database to yield significant results. For example, one might trace the number of firms in the various book trades over time, or map the locations of tradespeople's homes and workplaces, or study the disposition of places of business within the changing cityscape.[15]

e. City Directories and Census Materials

Many types of directory studies are based on city directories. These are fairly widely available on microform from the late 1700s down to 1935.[16] Although city directories do not include every tradesperson who was in business in a given year, they do give a sense of the local trade as it changes from year to year.

Manuscript census data offer more comprehensive information, but only for specific points in time—the weeks in a year during which the census was taken. Although decennial federal

data are accessible on microform at the various regional repositories of the National Archives and many research libraries, the
manuscripts for some years have been destroyed, and most of the
twentieth-century ones are closed because of privacy issues. The
very comprehensiveness of the population schedules means researchers must plow through reels of microfilm in search of
specific occupational titles. Yet studies of this sort are clearly
needed, especially for what they can say about the household
structures, age distributions, and patterns of geographical and
social mobility of people in the book trades. Many of the manuscript censuses have industrial schedules that make it relatively
simple to pinpoint specific book-trade firms and to compile information about their structure and even their finances (city or
state tax records can do the same). But there is also a wealth of
material appearing in print in the various digests that followed
most censuses after the mid-nineteenth century. Usually these
give a state-by-state breakdown of the trade, which allows for
quick comparisons to other industries.

f. Newspapers and Other Serials

Periodicals ranging from newspapers to monthly magazines or
expensive annuals provide another rich resource for book history, while at the same time they themselves are potential objects of study. Local newspaper advertisements often are the only
remaining evidence of some early American book-trade firms.
Advertisements by metropolitan publishers in small-town
newspapers suggest where those publishers thought their books
would sell.

There is an ocean of periodical material for researchers to sail
through. A few reference works provide excellent guides for the
voyage. Despite the high quality of this bibliographical control,
it is often difficult to gain access to this material. Full runs of
newspapers are surprisingly rare, even at the most specialized
research libraries. Some newspapers are available in microform,
especially for early America, but many later microform runs do
not circulate through interlibrary loan. To make matters worse,

indexes to newspapers are scarce. (The case for magazines is somewhat better than that for newspapers.)

g. Other Business/Public Sources

Book historians should be aware of sources in business history. Credit reports, bankruptcy notices, and court records can give important details about firms. Court records also may show the formation or dissolution of partnerships and incorporations. There are also federal records of various taxes paid on the importation or exportation of publications; like any other type of cargo, these items may appear in shipping lists. These sources make it easy to compare the book trades with other industries.

h. Conclusion

Most of these general sources remain untapped by book historians, and even in those areas where book historians have worked, there remains much to be done. Indeed, we are only at the beginning of the systematic study of the history of the book in the United States: buried still are not only many interesting and significant details about specific books, authors, publishers, printers, and the like, but also the larger picture of the pace, nature, and geography of the socioeconomic development of the American book trades.

2. GENRE-SPECIFIC SOURCES

The sources just discussed encompass many areas of the history of the book and present the field—especially publishing—more or less as a totality; however, much of the literature on the history of the book has been produced by scholars specializing in particular types or genres, and yet more remains to be done.

a. Trade Fiction and Poetry

Since the mid-nineteenth century trade fiction has contributed a large percentage of total book production and sales. Moreover, many, if not most, scholars of American literature focus on trade fiction, even though foreign authors, too, have been consistently popular with American readers.

American fiction publishing before 1900 is covered in Lyle Wright's *American Fiction,* published in the 1960s. Certainly many titles have emerged since he stopped work, but his bibliography covers most of the American-authored first-edition titles. Most items listed in *American Fiction* are reproduced in their entirety in a convenient microform edition. Bibliographical details on some of the principal titles can be found in Jacob Blanck's *Bibliography of American Literature* (1955–91).

A special feature of study in this area has been the best seller, which has been seen as a way to gauge national taste and to sample the "American mind." "Bestsellerdom" continually fascinates researchers and publishers alike who try to understand why one book sells and another does not. It should be remembered, however, that best sellers seldom sell a number of copies equal to more than one percent of the nation's population, and that percentage is not distributed evenly either across the American landscape or within social strata. Thus the relatively easy question of what books were best sellers must give way to the infinitely more difficult one of who actually read them.

No consideration of trade fiction would be complete without the paperback, which dates back to colonial "chapbooks"—cheap popular literature of all sorts, from fortune telling to religion to traditional medieval romances, perhaps mostly aimed at children. The first mass *fiction* paperback movement in the United States began in 1841, when *Brother Jonathan,* a story weekly, began to issue pamphlet supplements to speed up the clock of serial publication. Paperbacks declined around the turn of the twentieth century, but were brought back to life in the 1920s from the avant-garde and political left. The modern paperback revolution dates to 1939, when Pocket Books, Penguin Books (a British company), and other aggressive firms began to market paperbacks broadly and at low cost.

A related category, currently enjoying much popularity in both hardcover and paperback, is crime fiction. Allen J. Hubin's *Crime Fiction, 1749–1980* (1984) is the essential bibliographical guide here; it is unusually useful because of its indexes of settings and series. The long-lived popularity of the genre and its relationship to crime fact are questions that concern historians of the book.

Unlike crime literature, poetry has slid from its nineteenth-century high point. The verses of a poet like Henry Wadsworth Longfellow were once on the tongues of most Americans, and his books sold well. His and other writers' verse, of course, also appeared in periodicals, anthologies, and collections—vehicles with some continuing popularity.

Along with poetry, short fiction and nonfiction appeared in expensive gift books or annuals, which were often the top of the line for trade publishers in terms of price and presentation. The format began in the 1820s, hit its peak just before the Civil War—a rise chronicled in several good bibliographies—and then lost its distinctiveness amid a slew of other ornate or heavily illustrated books.

b. Trade Nonfiction

The large trade publishers have diversified lists that include fiction and an even greater range of nonfiction titles. In the history of the American publishing industry, nonfiction titles have far outnumbered fiction titles, but the work of literary scholars has made American fiction seem much more prominent than it actually is.

In the absence of a definitive bibliography of nonfiction, book historians have to make do with specific studies of the three most popular nonfiction genres: biography, history, and travel. Biographers' choice of subjects—models to emulate or, in the case of social outcasts, to avoid—have provided important guides to personal development in a socially and culturally open nation: little wonder that the genre has been a mainstay of publishing. Bibliographies of American history usually are geared toward current historical research and thus, ironically, do not usually take adequate account of history as a genre within larger, unfolding patterns of book production and reception. Finally, travel literature breaks down into several types of specialized bibliographies: those of works written by Americans abroad or at home (in particular, the westward pioneers); those of works by visitors to various spots in the United States or its territories; and—not to be forgotten because of their popularity throughout American history—those of narratives by writers of other nationalities about other countries. Relationships among the three nonfiction genres and with fiction provide virgin soil for book historians.

c. Children's Books

Unlike trade nonfiction, children's literature, both nonfiction and fiction, is a richly documented field with an extensive secondary-source literature. The period before 1821 is covered by a solid bibliography with a supporting microform collection.[7] A good union list (that is, a comprehensive list that combines holdings in various libraries) for the later period is still needed, but short of that, there are *Children's Books in Print* (1969–), several catalogs of important collections, an international directory of the catalogs, and, above all, an incisive and well-annotated guide to the subject put out by the Library of Congress.

d. Textbooks

Textbooks, at first glance, hold much in common with children's books because of their shared target audience. But their purchasers differ, for most of today's textbooks for primary and secondary schools are bought not by individuals but by schools or school systems.

Little work has been done in this area. A collection of 842 primers (small elementary reading instruction books) is available on microfiche with access through a guide. In 1985, the U.S. Office of Educational Research and Improvement issued a catalog of 6,108 of its holdings of American textbooks from

1775 to 1900. A comprehensive work, *American Educational Catalog,* has been published since 1872 and, for elementary and high school books, *El-Hi Textbooks and Serials in Print* since 1985, but this is not nearly enough. Most histories of schoolbooks focus on content and not upon the external details of production, distribution, and adoption. One external area, however, has received much scholarly attention—censorship. Overall, only a few sources, mostly histories of publishers, provide information from a history-of-the-book perspective.

e. Academic Books

Like textbook publishers, the publishers of academic books in hardcover today must reckon with a primarily institutional market, in this case, scholarly libraries (mostly for use by professors, graduate students, and disciplinary majors writing research papers). By contrast, paperback academic books are generally aimed for the classroom and, hence, are selected for adoption by college instructors. In academic publishing, they are more loosely related, for the former assumes a small market of specialists while the latter relies upon "course-adoptable" paperbacks that a wide array of students may find useful and that fit into standard college courses. Adoption decisions at the college level are usually made by individual instructors. Since what will sell, either to professionals or for classroom use, is always uncertain, most academic publishing has fallen to subsidized university presses.

Although academic publishing through university presses goes back to the Renaissance, it became important only in the late nineteenth century with the development of the modern research university. Unfortunately, there is no comprehensive bibliographical guide to this body of specialized information, so historians of the book must begin by assembling bibliographies from either *NUC* or on-line catalogs. Another approach is to build individual house histories from the ground up, for many university presses have retained some of their records. For example, one might focus on a particular scholar's work or the work of a group of scholars in order to trace patterns of intellectual influence.

f. Scientific, Technical, Medical, and Legal Books

Bibliographical control, both current and retrospective, is much better in specialized fields like science, technology, medicine, and law. These fields are related to scholarly publishing and sometimes overlap with it, and they have had a similar history.[18]

Science and technology were fundamental aspects of life in the young nation, and as a result both popular and specialist literature on such topics flourished. The very volume and diversity of such imprints present historians of the book with formidable problems, but good bibliographies and indexes do exist. Medical literature is especially well covered in bibliographies, though for some periods the coverage is not comprehensive, and a few works on medical publishers have appeared. Perhaps because of its self-referential and precedent-based nature, law is probably the most thoroughly treated area among these professional publications. There are also two large collections of American legal treatises after 1800 on microfilm.

g. Reference Books

Reference books may be distinguished from other types of works by the way readers use them: usually people do not read, or even skim, a reference work in its entirety, but rather search for an answer to a specific question. General reference works especially offer insight into the way people in the past "put their world together," for they supposedly are written at a basic level. Reference books have been among the steadiest selling yet least studied works of all genres in the United States. Robert Arner, in his 1991 work on America's first *Britannica,* at least made a start in exploring this area. The lack of scholarly interest is surprising given that adequate bibliographical control is available, especially for how-to guides. For example, two works cover cookbooks to 1860 and from 1860 to 1960, and there are some good bibliographies on such areas as sports literature. Finally, maps and atlases might also fall into this category of "consultable" works.

h. Religious Books

Religious publishing has been an important part of the book trade for so long that some book historians have used it as evidence of the centrality of the "Protestant vernacular" to American cultural life.[19] Indeed, one journalism historian, David Paul Nord, has controversially claimed that the modern American mass media had their origins in the early nineteenth-century evangelical press. This stands in marked contrast to the approach taken by many early twentieth-century historians of publishing, who equated the spread of printing with secularization. The pendulum swing away from this view has inspired much scholarly consideration of religious publishing of mainline Protestant denominations. This recent interest, however, has not yet led anyone to undertake an overall bibliography of the subject. The best grasp on the extensive periodical literature to 1830 can be found in Gaylord P. Albaugh's annotated bibliography (1994).

i. Business Books

The debate over the role of religious publishing has no counterpart in the business and economic press. Certainly, the outpouring of print from American business overwhelms that from the religious press. Output in this area is extremely diverse and—in the case of, say, printed wrappers and boxes or trade cards—expands the scope of the term "history of the *book*."

Some of the flavor of that diversity emerges in Henrietta M. Larson's *Guide to Business History* (1948) and David Forsyth's *Business Press in America, 1750–1860* (1964). A selected list of titles of company histories and business leaders' biographies has been assembled, and there is a retrospective of books from 1876 to 1983. The agricultural press has been considered in several works. There are individual studies of account books, advertising, bank note reporters, railroad books and periodicals, and trade cards and catalogs. But all sorts of common business-related materials, such as standard business forms and cards, ready reckoners, memorandum and blank books, credit reference books, and "businessmen's assistants," still await bibliographical scrutiny.

j. Specialty Publishing

Because of special production needs or specific systems of distribution, some publishers focus on only one type of imprint, from art books to greeting cards. Apart from some halting efforts aimed at collectors and aficionados, these types of imprints have been neglected, with one notable exception—sheet music. Even in this area, however, much work needs to be done on distribution and reception.

k. Other Private-Sector Publications

The United States has been called a nation of joiners, so it is no wonder that its rich associational life has spawned much published material. Learned societies played an important role in the development of early American science and higher learning. Historical societies, museums, private libraries, men's and women's clubs, think tanks, political parties, lobbyists, and advocacy groups are only a few kinds of voluntary associations that have acted as authors, publishers, and disseminators of books. To them should be added trade unions, although employers' associations are more accurately classed under business.

l. Government Publications

The public sector has generated an enormous and ever increasing amount of print over the centuries. Perhaps because of the need for public accountability for expenditures toward publication, bibliographic control is good for federal materials, fair for the states, but very poor for counties, municipalities, and smaller administrative units.

m. Translations and Imitations

Translations of European literature greatly influenced Americans during the early nineteenth century and again in the early twentieth century, especially in the hands of aggressive publishing entrepreneurs like Horace Liveright and the Boni brothers, who ushered in socially and morally "advanced" literature. Until recently, scholars of American literary reception have focused on original works, viewing foreign books as mere influences upon canonical American authors, and this may explain why, so far, little work has been done on translation publishing or even on attempts at imitation. UNESCO's *Index Translationum* provides some control back to 1932, but before that one must rely upon language-specific bibliographies.

n. Serials

We conclude this discussion of genre-specific sources with another area that, like translations, exists on the margins of book history for perhaps too many practitioners—serials. The reason for the distinction, it has been claimed, is that books are meant for long-term use and serials usually are not. Yet obviously this distinction breaks down under close scrutiny. Many books, like buyer's guides to stereo equipment, are designed for a limited shelf-life, and some types of serials, such as academic journals, publish research of lasting value. Some would argue that the periodicals that "count" over the long term eventually are bound in hard covers, but any review of library storage practices shows the arbitrariness of binding decisions. And any consideration of perishable materials preserved in alternative formats (like newspapers on microfilm) also undermines the notion that what is significant must be between covers. Perhaps another, better reason to distinguish book and serial publishing is the differences between the firms that publish them, though some firms, like Harper & Brothers, did both. The two types of firms diverge in their technologies of production, relations with authors, uses of advertising, and strategies of dissemination. These differences are real and cannot be ignored, yet little is gained by promoting the study of books as a more worthy endeavor than the study of serials.

We introduced the basic bibliographical guides to serials in our discussion of general sources, but there are more specific sources available. Many scholarly studies of newspapers have appeared in recent years that break with earlier approaches by paying attention to editors and writers, distribution, reception, and the business and social context of newspaperdom. There is also a rich literature on the nation's ethnic press and the perennial constitutional issue of freedom of the press. For entrée to primary sources for the study of newspapers, see the survey of newspaper archives and histories by the Newspaper History Task Force of the American Society of Newspaper Editors.

o. Conclusion

Clearly, there is great range and variance in the genres that have tumbled off America's presses. Any pathway through a genre provides ample opportunities to study book history, but there is also a need for comparative genre studies and, especially, for a synthesis of all genres. Indeed, one of the greatest hindrances to the study of the book in the United States has been a lack of uniform series of data that can be analyzed in various ways to provide an overall picture.

B. PRODUCERS

Many book historians look beyond imprint-based sources to unravel the processes and personalities involved in print production—to explore the parentage, so to speak, of books and periodicals and their early environments. Imprints, like people, are shaped by their genealogy and place of birth. It would make a lifeless work indeed to leave out such important shaping influences.[20]

1. WRITERS' PERSONAL AND PROFESSIONAL PAPERS

Some historians of the book, especially literary specialists, consider authors to be the most essential component of book production. Authors are, of course, the ultimate source of texts, but they write with audiences in mind. Further, their words are subject to intervention by publishers, editors, and printers before they ever reach the public. In this way, authorship is inseparable from readership or the book trades, since autonomy is more the ideal than the reality for authors. Many book historians study the interplay of the author's creative wellsprings with more mundane, material factors of the literary marketplace.[21] While literary critics help us to appreciate an author's text for its aesthetic qualities, book historians weigh the historical forces that had an impact on an author's production. Put another way, the concept and practice of authorship exist within a historical context, even though great literature is itself, as some would argue, timeless. Below, we sketch this evolving historical context and refer to the relevant scholarship that has made use of authors' papers and other biographical material to understand the changing vocation of authorship in the United States. We conclude with a few pointers about where to look for such papers.

"Authorship" for book historians usually, but by no means always, equates with professionalism—that is, authors who did not write for free.[22] When William Charvat wrote in 1954 that "the genius or talent of a newly emergent group of writers is one thing; the transformation of genius into books which provide a living for the geniuses is quite another," he was summing up the future of authorship studies for decades to come.[23] One focus of authorship has been the birth of "professionalization," the change over time from gentleman (seldom woman) of leisure or recipient of patronage, who decried the very idea of being paid for his work, to a man or woman who depended upon publishers, markets, and audiences to help him or her earn a living primarily from writing. Charvat traced this sequence using a variety of sources, including authors' journals, memoirs, and correspondence (especially with publishers). He looked at some of the monetary exchanges that took place, such as payment for a property, royalties (the percentage an author gets from a sale), and the author's ability to have control over a creation by owning the plates for reprinting or gaining protection from copyright law. He also examined larger factors, culled from secondary sources, that helped explain why the transformation could take place: a wider reading audience with more disposable income, broader distribution of books, rapid development of transportation systems, and the increasing impact of economic shifts.[24]

Where do women—the minority of authors, who through most of American history have been discouraged from earning money in the public world of writing—fit into authorship studies? Scholars have delved into women's biographies as well as the cultural forces that shaped their gendered roles, in order to understand female authorship. Lawrence Buell's prosopography of New England authors—a group portrait based upon biographical data—shows that economic necessity determined women's decision to professionalize at least as much as men's. But women authored books under quite different cultural circumstances, such as the "woman's sphere" or the "cult of true womanhood"—the constructs that relegated women to domesticity in the nineteenth century.[25]

Mary Kelley, who constructed several biographies from the personal papers of women writers (for example, Caroline Lee Hentz and Maria Cummins), concluded that they should be called "literary domestics": active both on the public stage of authorship and in the private realm within the home that inspired them to write.[26] The notion of the "woman's sphere" prevented them from being seen in their own day as equal to male authors, in terms of the quality of their work. Susan Coultrap-McQuin, however, notes that more privatized authorship was genderless, since it was compatible with older, seventeenth-century ideals of gentlemanly writing for self-edification, not pay. Yet women were as astute as men in understanding the business of publishing, even as it was losing traces of gentility after the Civil War; for example, Mary Abigail Dodge's stormy dealings in letters to her publisher James T. Fields and her account in *Battle of the Books* (1870) are testament enough to her professionalism.[27]

In order to understand better the trend toward professionalism, historians of the book focus upon authorship before the time when writers could depend upon their work to support themselves—that is, before the 1820s.[28] Although they were not "professionals" in the modern sense, authors nonetheless existed during the eighteenth century, although many were anonymous or took part in collaborative efforts (*The Federalist* [1787–88] is a good example).[29] For those who signed their individual efforts, there was little protection from plagiarism or seriously altered reprintings. These early American writers often solicited subscribers, or people who promised to buy the work once it was printed (see the discussion on readers, below). But many American researchers focus less upon the cash transactions than upon the larger cultural and historical forces that influenced a particular author's output. Some scholars, for example, debate whether or not the birth in the late seventeenth century of the "public sphere," a space away from state and civic control (like coffeehouses or literary salons), allowed authors to be critical of existing forms of government (monarchy) and thus to contribute to an "enlightened" ideology of republicanism. Other scholars investigate such questions as whether or not the "spirit of capitalism" and liberalism in the early republic spurred authors on toward professionalism.[30]

Most recently, focus has turned toward the reading public or audience as an important component of an author's impulse to create. As Charvat realized, although "it has been recognized often enough that the relation between the writer and society is reciprocal," still "we need more demonstration."[31] Scholars have answered that call by studying how authors perceived their audience through the lens of their culture and literary marketplace, rather than focusing on the privatized encounter that takes place through individuals' readings of published texts. Of course, an author's notions of audience can be discerned in his or her published works, especially in historical genres; for example, Benjamin Franklin's *Autobiography* assumes a democratic posture toward everyman as potential author of his own life.[32] Further, solid evidence can be found in an author's direct or implied statements about readership. Stephen Railton noted that for authors of the American Renaissance, "audience was almost palpably present when they sat down to write." He looked at authors' published memoirs, their essays on literature, and prefaces to their own works in which they often directly addressed the perceived audience. But the reading public could be "also an abstraction imagined in response to the romantic writers' professional frustrations with the literary institutions of the nineteenth century"—one that resisted conforming to an author's misinformed expectations.[33]

Some of that misapprehension, as can be seen throughout authors' correspondence, doubtless derived from the celebrity a few European, and especially British, authors had attained as geniuses who created and sustained their own public. Indeed, as some recent scholars have shown, writers like Byron or Walter Scott contributed to conceptions of Anglo-American cultural identity and became touchstones for literary comparisons on both sides of the Atlantic. Strident literary nationalists of the Jacksonian era naturally called for an American counterpart to these foreign geniuses. Though none of comparable stature emerged, a few writers, like Henry Wadsworth Longfellow, did manage to achieve the ubiquity attending such fame, a phenomenon that was perpetuated, in Longfellow's case, by schoolroom recitation exercises down through the early decades of the twentieth century.

The literary nationalism of the antebellum years did help make American literature less provincial. The English wit Sydney Smith had asked snidely, "Who reads an American book?" In effect, this question was answered by a transformation in the nationality of authorship. At the start of the nineteenth century, foreign writers wrote the vast majority of books read by Americans, but by the 1850s Americans accounted for about half of the authorship.[34] The nationalization of authorship is even more remarkable given a simple economic reality of the day: in the absence of international copyright, a British author's work could be pirated for free, while American copyright law protected native authors and left open the possibility that they might get paid.

Of course, ideology alone does not account for the Americanization of authorship, for such literary nationalist calls have only very rarely resulted in a local literary florescence in cultural provinces or colonies. There were at least two other causes: cutthroat competition and special market needs. Intense American competition for British reprints unprotected by copyright led some publishers to turn to protected, American-authored literary properties. The American market increasingly demanded schoolbooks dealing with national geography, history, and civics, and general books with relevant, newsworthy content—such as Harriet Beecher Stowe's 1852 runaway best seller, *Uncle Tom's Cabin*.[35]

The success of Stowe's book suggests a new emphasis in celebrity by the mid-nineteenth century, one based on sales. In a culture that increasingly worshiped financial gain as a sign of greater moral worth, mastery of the market, especially by authors who had started out poor, made best-selling authors one more chapter in the great American success story. Celebrity was also underscored by stereotyping—a process in which an impression was taken of typeset matter and then used to create plates from which future editions could be easily printed. Such a permanent form of capitalizing the considerable costs of initial typesetting led publishers to encourage authors to develop long careers. The reputation of American authors was further enhanced by newspaper and magazine editors, who, always hungry for copy, appropriated snippets of some popular writers' work and then, late in the nineteenth century, contributed to the professionalization of authorship by paying authors, sometimes handsomely, for the work. The vibrant magazine market, fueled by literary syndicates, particularly benefited American authors when the 1891 Copyright Act diminished international literary piracy. Authorship could now pay well, at least for the artful and the lucky.

The result was a curious blend of artist, craftsperson, and entrepreneur. Michael Anesko has noted the effect of the situation upon Henry James: "James anxiously desired to reach a mass audience at the same time that he remained suspicious of it; the hopes—and fears—that he associated with the fate of his literary commodity in the public sphere become translated into fictional parables of exposure."[36] In short, many writers not only wrote for the market, but also incorporated the anxiety they felt about it into their work.

By the turn of the twentieth century some prominent authors reacted to the insecurities of the market with further professionalization. According to Christopher P. Wilson, these writers coolly deployed "standard devices of popular romance" to achieve naturalistic ends. Authors like Jack London or Upton Sinclair became writing experts, able to produce intellectual products that publishers deemed ever reliable in the marketplace.[37] The inventors of modern American literary professionalism bequeathed to their successors a technical approach to authorship, as witnessed by the many writer's handbooks and creative writing workshops that have flourished since the Progressive Era.[38] The trend developed further in the period between the two world wars, as can be seen in the professional practice of Ernest Hemingway: his manuscripts testify to his reduction of initial Victorian excess to streamlined modernist prose—achieved through tight professional editing.[39] At the same time the rapid commercial development of publishing, centered in New York City, permitted a class of roving intellectuals, like Edmund Wilson or Van Wyck Brooks, to survive.

Since World War II, with the rapid development of institutions of higher learning in the United States and the rise of a culture of credentialism, professional authorship has increasingly entered into a symbiotic relationship with academe. Universities now provide training in all types of writing and provide authors with credentials that allow them to claim some area of expertise. Success in publication, in turn, may help authors who work in university settings advance in their profession. And, of course, that employment can sustain authors between projects and offer a range of benefits besides.[40]

The best way to trace this course of authorship from gentleman amateur to worker/technician is through authors' papers. Such papers can encompass personal correspondence as well as various types of manuscript material used in writing for publication, along with the succession of drafts that usually accumulate as a manuscript develops (these drafts are treated separately, below). Strewn throughout these papers may be receipts, contracts, and other financial or legal material that can give keen insight into an author's life and working methods. Some of the material may be in the author's own handwriting; this type of manuscript is usually called a *holograph*.

For all authors, the obvious first place to look for this type of material is in the bibliographies and notes of biographies and critical studies of specific authors. The bibliographies in the relevant volumes of the *Dictionary of Literary Biography* provide glimpses into the literature on various authors. Bibliographies about specific prominent authors should also be consulted. The correspondence of some well-known writers has been published under the auspices of the Center for Scholarly Editions of the Modern Language Association. The center oversees its editing projects and requires that they observe the highest bibliographical standards.[41]

Of course, these printed materials are but the tip of an iceberg of manuscript sources available. Even for prominent authors, published correspondence is seldom complete or comprehensive regarding letters sent to the individual. Access to the manuscript materials of many authors, including some obscure ones, is provided by J. Albert Robbins in his *American Literary Manuscripts* (1977). Some archives that specialize in authors' manuscripts, like the Huntington Library in San Marino, California, the Berg Collection at the New York Public Library, and the Harry L. Ransom Center at the University of Texas, have published catalogs of their holdings. Of course, not all authors' manuscript material is found in collections devoted to them; in addition, it is often necessary to probe into the collections of people who were associated with them in some way, in hopes that letters to them might have survived.

Authors' papers can be the springboard for several different types of projects. For example, letters may suggest the author's attitudes toward specific publishers, agents, authors, and professionalization in general. It might be possible to discover which of an author's books brought the highest royalties over what period of time. The tone or style of letters may be compared to the author's published work to understand the differences in representation between the private person and the public author.

2. LITERARY AGENTS

Literary agents are the middlemen (and women) between authors and publishers in more ways than one. They are not only a conduit between the two but also share some of their qualities. Writers, when they begin writing a book for an audience or a market, are in essence making decisions about what could sell, just as an agent does. Publishers, when they screen manuscripts for marketability, also act like agents. Most of all, literary agents are involved with the flood of paperwork that surrounds the negotiations of writers and other cultural producers. That paperwork, as we will see, can be a boon to researchers: it conveniently represents both sides of the author/publisher interaction, and it often contains some frank exchanges.[42]

Unfortunately, there is no guide to manuscript collections of literary agents. Further, it is hard to link agents with particular books, except through authors' acknowledgments. The chitchat in trade journals like *Publishers Weekly* can provide hints, but otherwise the researcher must rely upon evidence in the papers of authors and publishers in order to find a lead. Once the agent has been discovered, a run through the *National Union Catalog of Manuscript Collections* (1959–63) might reveal specific collections for agents; short of this, there are some published reminiscences of agents.[43]

3. PUBLISHERS

Before publishing emerged as a separate business in the early nineteenth century, it was closely allied to printing. Publishers began to focus on acquiring manuscripts from authors, editing them, coordinating the details of the jobbers who produced the books, marketing the books, and distributing royalties to authors.

Because publishers make the basic decisions of whether to turn a manuscript into a book, what form it should take, and how and to whom it should be marketed, they have been dubbed "gatekeepers" between authorial creativity and readers.[44] In truth, writers are not so unworldly, nor are readers so passive. The gatekeeper concept suggests a supply-side assumption—if you print enough books there will be plenty of people to buy them—that is simply not borne out by the many books which remain unsold.

Despite (or because of) their importance in providing the public with literature for profit, publishers have too often been stereotyped as grasping, venal philistines who simply never really understand the author, the book, or the market eager to buy the book. Doubtless some publishers fit the mold, but probably no more so than executives who traffic in other aspects of culture.

a. Printed Secondary Materials

Although no comprehensive, retrospective directory of American publishers has been compiled, specific periods and cities are covered by the book-trade directories mentioned earlier and by other standard sources. In addition to such standard sources, there is a variety of more specialized sources, which we discuss in turn, below.

i. Firm histories and biographies. Firm histories and publisher biographies must be approached with a critical eye, for many are written by people so involved in the industry that their involvement may color what they have to say. Still, in-house works can be of considerable value, for in many instances they supply all the information that exists about obscure firms.[45] Independent scholarly histories of publishing houses are surprisingly scarce relative to the number of houses that have come and gone—this despite an abundance of raw material in print.[46]

ii. Advertising. Publication advertisements give clues to publishers' intentions and activities. As early as the mid-nineteenth century, such solicitations achieved considerable sophistication in terms of psychological appeals and the development of advertising campaigns.[47] The advertisements come in several forms. Book prospectuses, many of which still exist, were often circulated as a means of generating enough revenue, through subscriptions or pre-publication orders, to publish the book. Publisher-financed advertising (as opposed to seemingly free "notices" by the editor) in periodicals, especially local ones, is a generally accessible resource, though posters are rare.[48]

iii. Lists of house titles. One of the quickest and simplest ways to get an overview of a publishing house and its development is to assemble, from advertisements or from the general bibliographical sources discussed above, a chronological list of every title the house produced. These lists should be the backbone of any study of a house's history, for they record the series of entrepreneurial decisions made in rough order and suggest how the firm responded to its successes and failures.

b. Business Papers

Like many other modern businesses, publishing houses generate much internal paperwork that is usually preserved only while it is useful. Useless paperwork may accumulate, of course, but is vulnerable to all sorts of circumstances: housecleaning, moves to other properties, or absorption by other firms. Nevertheless, to find the rare instance of an accessible publisher's archive is to hit pay dirt, so to speak, for at once a rich perspective on book history comes into full view, one that encompasses not only the many players involved in producing a book, but also disseminators and even, at times, readers and other consumers. A solid guide by Beth Luey and colleagues, *A Guide to Book Publishers' Archives* (1996), provides access to some of this material. Of course, to use this material researchers must visit manuscript archives in person and work through boxes of material often only organized at the collection level.

The archives of a few important publishers, however, do appear in microform editions.

i. Author files. In many of these archives the richest lode of information, and often the one most likely to be preserved, is the house's correspondence with its authors. The quality of this correspondence differs from house to house and author to author, of course, but even in seemingly humdrum exchanges, one may gain flashes of insight into the self-representations and motivations of publishers and authors. Recently this type of correspondence has been appearing in print.

ii. Contracts. Another type of document likely to appear in publishers' archives is the contracts struck with authors and subsidiary rights publishers (contracts with jobbers show up less often). This is obviously not as rich a source as correspondence, for most publisher-author arrangements tend to follow a standardized contract; however, such contracts can become important, complex, and unique for best-selling authors.[49]

iii. Accounts. Publishers, like other businesspeople, kept track of their affairs. The various ledgers, daybooks, waste books, journals, order books, subscription lists, and cost books contain an amount of quantitative information that can be daunting and confusing. Happily, the data can be entered into a computer and analyzed to answer significant questions: How well did the house do over time? What books sold better than others and in what regions, towns, or cities did they do so? How much did authors make from successful or unsuccessful books, compared to the house's profits?[50]

c. Editorial Services

Obviously, the relationship between publishers and authors involves textual editing as one important element. The text that is used for typesetting, and even the typeset material itself before the press run, is subject to considerable negotiation. Sometimes the house merely ensures stylistic consistency and correct usage, a process called line editing or copy editing. But at its higher levels, editing becomes something of a collaboration with the author, as the editor gives direction about the manuscript as a whole, offers suggestions for restructuring, and deletes entire portions or recommends that new ones be added. Not surprisingly, this series of textual negotiations leaves a paper trail—a boon for historians of the book.

i. Copy-edited manuscripts. Among the richest elements of the paper trail is the original, edited text with editorial markings upon it. From this we can reconstruct part of the give-and-take of editing, as editors try to rid the work of blunders, for mistakes and vagaries inevitably creep in, even, and perhaps especially, in the original.

ii. Galleys and proofs. Typeset material is made following the copy-edited manuscript and goes through yet more alteration, which historians of the book may recover. Before electronic photocomposition, typeset text was assembled in an oblong case called a galley, from which a test imprint without page formatting was made on a long sheet of paper. The result was called a galley proof, which was proofread in the shop by the printers, but also at times by editors and authors.

iii. Editor-author correspondence. The letters that pass between editor and author obviously resemble the correspondence between publisher and author, as discussed above. Exchanges with editors, however, often go beyond their role in acquiring suitable and marketable manuscripts to focus more on giving the text its final shape. In fact, analysis of copy-edited manuscripts and galleys, when combined with a full run of author-editor correspondence, can yield a multi-layered picture of production practices and social relations.

iv. Editorial biography. Finally, there are some editors, mostly in the twentieth century, whose work and life have come out of the shadows of authors and who have themselves been the subject of biographies. Published biographies of such editorial titans as Maxwell Perkins and Saxe Commins point the way for considering how the lives and careers of lesser-known editors, both of books and periodicals, may have shaped the course of American literary history.

4. PRINTERS

Printers did not always limit their role to producing the unbound sheets that make up the book. Before the mid-nineteenth century, printers might also act as editors, typesetters, publishers, binders, advertisers, library proprietors, and booksellers.[51] The industrialization of printing has its own fascinating story to tell, for printing was among the first trades to undergo the transformation, making it the original "culture industry."[52]

a. Ledgers and Other Business Papers

Various printers' manuscript ledgers and other business papers have survived.[53] Daybook ledgers usually contain, under the date of the transaction, the name of the customer, the price of the service rendered, and strikethroughs of paid debts. Account books can also conveniently portray the overall economic health of the enterprise. Time books of industrial firms can testify to the persistence of the labor pool for one employer, seasonality of work, or daily to monthly patterns of hiring. Unfortunately, given the often dry and tedious nature of this material, most of it remains in manuscript form.[54]

b. Personal Papers

The personal papers of printers offer a different, less quantitative kind of insight. David Clapp Jr., for example, recorded in his diary for 22 May 1822, "I went to Mr. John Cottons Jr. in Boston to learn the printers trade. Terms 2,50 per week for my board $10 and the privilege of doing jobs for the first year." The end of the entry reveals the entrepreneurial space often cut for artisans in these shops: they could earn extra money on the side by taking on their own jobs. At the end of that year, when economic difficulty caused his employer to dismiss all his help but Clapp, he joked, "I still continue to work alone, with nobody but the mice, who scamper around the silent office as if they thought it had been deserted on purpose to oblige them."[55] These personal papers can also convey the horrors of industrial accidents, as in the case of Clapp's son, whose hand was mangled in the press, as described by his sister:

> When John came home tonight ∧ ^he^ had his hand all bandaged up, and, he said that ∧ ^he jammed three fingers^ ~~it~~ in the printing press, very badly, so as to make him vomit some. When father was putting the poultice on, when he got home it made him vomit again, and I was afraid I should faint away, so I went down stairs, and felt faint a little. Mother was so faint that she had to go and lie down, and Mary felt rather faint too.

Nine days later she reveals that the accident resulted in a permanent impression: "the type went on to ~~John's~~ ^his^ fingers, and printed some letters on one of them." This printer, tragically, had become his own imprint, so to speak.[56]

Despite the wealth of insight these personal sources offer, no one has yet undertaken the task of assembling a list of available manuscript or print items by printers. The best approach to finding these sources is through some of the classic works of printing history.

c. Manuals

The print industry has produced many "how-to" manuals that reveal past shop practices and trade problems. C. S. Van Winkle's *The Printer's Guide* (1827), for example, tells apprentices how they should stand and gives detailed directions about distributing type back into cases, as well as about composing and imposition (the way different pages are oriented on large sheets so that they come right when folded and cut). The manuals also speak to master printers, for example, warning them against hiring runaway apprentices. Sometimes manuals provide technical information, such as tables to calculate the amount of paper required to print a book. Such manuals may be located by consulting a few specialized lists as well as the printers' library catalogs cited below.

d. Type Specimen Books

Rarer than printers' manuals but offering unique information are type specimen books. Both typefoundries and printers produced these advertising samples of their work. The most common use of the type specimen books by historians is to help estimate the publication date of undated imprints. These specimens also provide a vocabulary for book historians who wish to describe and analyze typography. These books occasionally provide hints about the suggested uses of specific types for certain kinds of texts.

e. Artifacts

One may read about press operations and experience the look of presswork, but an encounter with the physical artifacts of printing has an impact all its own. There are several fine collections of artifacts available—for example, those of the National Museum of American History, Washington, D.C., and the Henry Ford Museum, Dearborn, Michigan. Artifacts range from composing sticks to power-driven presses and typesetting machines. Some living-history museums, like Old Sturbridge Village, Colonial Williamsburg, and New York's South Street Seaport Museum, maintain their own period print shops, which give demonstrations of the art.

f. Biographies and Firm Histories

Published biographies and firm histories of printers come in several varieties. There are a few collective biographies, starting with Isaiah Thomas's in 1810, but the field later becomes so vast that the only works that can claim to be comprehensive are local. Reminiscences, especially those of nineteenth-century figures, often resemble the collective biographies in treating a group of printers and other book-trade people at some length. Full-length autobiographies are more frequent for the twentieth century and, as is the case with most autobiographical material, must be approached with a critical eye. Biographies of printers who remained in the trade are few, although those of people who moved on to fame in other areas, like Benjamin Franklin and Henry George, are common. No comprehensive bibliographical source currently provides access to the various types of published accounts by or of individuals.

g. Trade Unions and Employers' Organizations

Labor unions came earlier to printing than to most trades. Strikes date back to the late eighteenth century, and by the early 1830s, printers' unions were forming, such as the Typographical Association of New York. Many of the documents originating from this period are reprinted in Ethelbert Stewart's *Documentary History of Early Labor Organizations of Printers* (1905). The unions grew up alongside employers' organizations and, apart from obvious points of difference, actually shared a concern with security and a related worry about overcompetition. After an abortive attempt to found a national union just before the Panic of 1837, the National Typographic Union was formed in 1852. But a natural rift developed between compositors, whose work remained craft-based, and the pressmen, whose work was increasingly mechanized. As a result, in 1889 the pressmen formed their own organization, the International Printing Pressmen's Union. The old and the new unions alternately feuded and attempted to cooperate, and then in 1911 the two were reunited with other, similar trades in the International Allied Printing Trades Association. The best access to information about these organizations is through their various publications.

5. OTHER

Authors, agents, publishers, editors, and printers are only the most obvious producers of books and periodicals—perhaps because they are involved in one way or another in the production of texts more than artifacts, or so it seems. But, as we will see, there are many other important contributors to the production of the printed word.

a. Typefoundries

The United States long remained dependent on Europe for metal type, despite the establishment, by Archibald Binny and James Ronaldson, of the first true American typefoundry in

Philadelphia in 1796. This was followed by similar efforts by David and George Bruce in New York and by the Boston Type and Stereotype Foundry. Only with the industrialization of typography, through electrotypography, lithography, and finally linotypography, did Americans achieve independence in this area, although the local wood-type trade flourished. By the early twentieth century, typefounding was becoming type design, and eventually offset printing ended metal letterpressing.

The evidence available for typefoundries consists of three basic sorts: (1) type specimen books (mentioned earlier in regard to printers); (2) foundry advertising in both trade and general newspapers; and (3) manuscript collections of business papers of these firms.[57]

b. Illustrators

Like typefounding, book illustration was revolutionized by the successive waves of innovation in typographical reproduction that swept through the nineteenth century. Before that, illustrations were printed from either wood blocks or copperplate; with the advent of stereotyping, illustrations were placed along with text in that form.

Unlike typefounding, which was a hardware-intensive industry, most of the human energy in illustration went into drawing or engraving. Hence, book historians have been most interested in these producers and their work, and less so in the processes used to bring that work before the public. Several lists of engravers exist to help book historians in this area, and there is a growing literature on the twentieth-century successor to drawn illustrations—photographic illustration.

c. Bookbinders

Before the mid-nineteenth century the covers and sheets of books were produced separately; placing a cover on the book was the responsibility of the book buyer. Bookbinding was a tedious process that could consume a craftsman's full day for but a single volume. This limited the number of books that could be

bound in any given community, yet the craft was so individualized that some historians can link bindings, just by their look, to
particular craftspeople. By the mid-nineteenth century a series
of innovations led to so-called edition binding, a uniform look
for all copies produced, while mechanization allowed binderies
to proliferate.

d. Papermakers

Papermaking is somewhat independent from other book trades.
While much paper output goes to book and periodical production, a good deal goes to allied trades in which printing takes a
secondary role: stationery, containers, wrappers, cards, or wallpaper, to name a few. It is important to remember, too, that the
history of paper goes back much further than that of movable
type—all the way back to A.D. 105 in China, when disintegrated
fiber was first used to produce a flexible and relatively inexpensive writing surface. Eventually macerated rags became the
characteristic ingredient of early modern European paper production; in the early nineteenth century, with the advent of
mechanized paper production, the rags gave way to increasing
content of much less durable wood pulp.[58] Papermakers often
literally left their mark on their products, by impressing the wet
paper while it was still in the mold with a design unique to the
manufacturer. The resulting slight difference in paper thickness
where the design was impressed is called a watermark. The
watermark can be easily viewed by holding the sheet of paper
up to a source of light. Retrospective catalogs of watermarks are
increasingly available and allow researchers to link specific paper
to specific manufacturers and dates of production with uncanny
precision. Such sources offer many opportunities for book historians to unravel the histories not only of paper manufacturing
firms but also of distributors and retailers. Through a combination of work in city directories, scans of newspaper
advertisements, and manuscript census records, a composite
picture of this aspect of book history can be built up.

6. BOOKS AS ARTIFACTUAL AND DOCUMENTARY EVIDENCE

The history of texts can be traced through the study of their physical properties as books. This study is known as *bibliography*. The term is often defined simplistically; for example, we tend to think of a bibliography as a list of titles pertaining to a certain subject, as in the list of works cited at the end of a scholarly book or even a longer catalog of titles, published separately, on a topic or time period. This kind of compilation is usually called *enumerative bibliography*. But we are concerned here with *descriptive bibliography*, which is actually the product of rigorous study intended to aid literary critics in their quest for an author's ideally intended text. Descriptive bibliographers help textual and literary critics by attempting to reconstruct the journey of a book from a pristine form ("the ideal copy as the printer intended it to leave his hands") through its various subsequent editions and printings. This kind of bibliographer describes each edition or variant, against the prototype, as carefully as possible—enough so that a reader of the bibliography can almost envision the format, page by page, of each variant of the book. This is done in a form of notation (especially formulated for early books) made exact by W. W. Greg and, later, Fredson Bowers.[59] Most book historians never aspire to the standards set by these bibliographers, one of whom acknowledged that descriptive bibliography's "general effects tend more to show the specialist what he does not yet know than to open up new territory for exploitation by the general scholar."[60]

What is of greater use for most persons interested in book history is an understanding of *analytical bibliography*—the study of the physical properties of books, upon which descriptive bibliographers base their work. Every book contains a whole vocabulary of signs that reflect upon its passage from handwritten or typescript manuscript to its first published form, and then into subsequent editions, variants, or states. These signs are apparent if one reads the book not for its meaning or story line, but instead for its physical properties. To look at a book for its binding (it is permissible in this case to judge a book by its cover!), the typeface used, or the paper on which the type printed the words, is to perform the work of an analytical bibliographer. The earliest books (called *incunabula*)—few people indeed are ever lucky enough to hold one in their hands for examination—give signs, such as the colophon, that are usually absent in modern books. The name of the printer and the date of completion often appear at the end of these early printed texts. Early books also contain "signatures"—not autographs, but directions (running vertically at the bottom of pages) to the bookbinder for folding the printed paper that makes up the pages in a book. Besides these features, there are also signs of wear and tear, for it is inevitable and even desirable that "humankind make their own books, then they begin to use them up."[61]

More modern books will not bear many of the signs of the oldest books, such as signatures or colophons, but much information still appears on the title page and its verso, commonly called the copyright page. Title pages can be analyzed for the decorative forms they sometimes take, replete with engravings, photographs, or other artistic embellishment. Like older books, modern books—even in the era of electronic typesetting—use various forms of typeface, such as roman, italic, and gothic, each with its own merits; some are more readable or simply more attractive than others. Look at some nineteenth-century print, especially advertisements in newspapers or magazines, and notice the standard forms of typeface, often elaborately embellished. Binding techniques too have changed since the post–World War II "paperback revolution" of affordable books with pages glued into paper covers. Still, many older books and some new ones are handsewn and bound in expensive and decorative leather cases. Perhaps the most pervasive sign within a modern book is the copyright symbol (©) and accompanying date on the verso of the title page. This is a relatively new addition, based upon copyright laws that protect authors' materials. Another is the Cataloging-in-Publication data, printed beneath the copyright information, which helps catalogers find a place for the book among others of its kind in a modern library setting. Still another is the infinity symbol (∞), used by some university presses to indicate that a book has been printed upon acid-free (longer lasting) paper.

Analytical bibliography can spur studies based upon the book's physical properties—studies that reach beyond the end product of a descriptive bibliography. One bibliographer, for example, calls for more analysis of the material forms of books and their "expressive function in conveying meaning." In other words, how does the appearance of a text affect our reading of it? An author's intended meaning can be subject to intervention as much by the publisher's choice of typography, paper, and other "bibliographical signs," as by editing or printer's changes. In this way human intervention affects the author's production and alters its original meaning.[62] Other scholars have studied changes in the "packaging" of authors' texts from the perspective of the publishers of the modern era, when "utility, not magnificence, is the criterion" for mass-producing affordable yet profit-making books. One might also explore the conditions under which publishers created expensive, elaborate gift books that bestowed status on recipients, or called attention to the fine typeface of a periodical to advertise its genteel character.[63]

7. BOOKS AND THE LAW

Law provides an important context for the printed word in the United States. It can protect the property of authors and publishers, but it also places limits upon what can be put into print. Legislation governs the flow of print from outside the nation, as well as the flow of American products abroad.

a. Copyright

The U.S. government's efforts to protect intellectual property have made copyrighting an important part of book history. From the 1790s on, publishers and/or authors have sought, by registering their work with the U.S. Copyright Office, to use federal law to protect themselves from plagiarism or outright theft by Americans. (Only with the international copyright agreement of 1891 did some protections extend overseas.) The records of the Copyright Office thus contain important information that can help date undated works or identify the author of anonymous works; in some cases, the copyright record is all that is left to testify to a book's existence (though not all copyright works were indeed printed).[64] Court records and briefs of federal cases arising out of copyright disputes are a rich, yet mostly untapped, source for book historians.

b. Censorship

In 1690 the first newspaper published in the British American colonies, Boston's *Publick Occurrences, Both Foreign and Domestic,* was suppressed by the government after but one issue. This marked the beginning of a long and continuing struggle to balance, on the one hand, the desire of authorities to maintain the public peace or welfare through censorship with, on the other, the press's and publishing industry's drive to bring before the public even disturbing or erroneous materials if they seemed likely to find an audience or if someone simply wished to finance such a venture. Book historians can trace these various struggles over press and book censorship through the discourse surrounding specific issues in the periodical literature and in the debates in governmental bodies (for example, those surrounding federal sedition legislation in 1798 and 1917–18). Insight can equally be gained from the court reports of various cases involving censorship at all levels of government. Finally, surveillance of authors by government agencies has produced an unintentionally fertile source for the history of the book.

c. Foreign Trade

Perhaps because most literary historians' interests have stopped at national borders, fairly little attention has been paid by Americans to the nuts and bolts of the international book trade after the colonial period. While some work has been done on international copyright legislation, protectionism—especially as expressed in U.S. tariffs on imports not only of imprints but also of the raw materials of the book trade—is an even more important but generally overlooked theme. U.S. Customs records, ship registers, and the debates in Congress surrounding the tariff can supply the primary-source information for book historians working in this area. It must be remembered, however, that trade went two ways: the policies and practices of nations receiving American imprints must also be examined.

8. CONCLUSION

Clearly, more individuals and corporate entities are involved in producing books than just authors and publishers. Fundamental control of the processes that produce meaning through printed texts is shared by many players, who may at times play at cross-purposes or simply by different rules. Hence, a book, magazine, or newspaper does not usually emerge from the publishing house as a product with a single meaning intended by one producer; rather, it is more often the site of multiple meanings, or multivalency, contested at times by authors, agents, publishers, editors, and other players.

C. DISSEMINATORS

Once a book leaves a publisher's warehouse, it is "finished" in material terms, but it is not yet, culturally speaking, a finished product. It has still to go through many more interventions that select and shape the channels through which the book will ultimately be received.

I. DISTRIBUTORS

Distributors are middlemen in the transit of books from publishers to consumers. They warehouse books, handle orders, and arrange for shipping. Because they handle books from several publishers—and the distributors employ economies of scale that lead them to become virtual monopolies, like the American News Company—they provide a unique vantage point. For book historians, the business papers of distributors can be very useful, since they assemble in one place the destinations of a variety of publications.

2. RETAILERS

Perhaps the moment in the dissemination process that has the strongest impact upon the consumer is at the point of sale. At this point, the consumer takes in information that helps contextualize the meaning of the book. The location of a book on the shelves is the main indicator of meaning in a bookstore. For example, a quasi-autobiographical novel about one woman's quest for spiritual growth might, depending on the bookstore, be displayed among fiction, biography, religion, New Age, or women's studies. The shelf location helps shape the purchaser's expectations of the book and, thus, contributes to the meaning he or she may find in it. But shelf location is not all: salespeople's advice, or the social types of shoppers hovering in the area where the book is displayed, are only a few of several other factors introduced into the production of meaning.

a. Booksellers

Bookshops have historically been the place where most consumers encounter books. These retail venues have two related lineages: general stores and printing shops, both of which sold books down through the nineteenth century. Unfortunately, much romance surrounds the bookstores of yore (especially in the nineteenth century), and historians have simply not taken the stores very seriously, except perhaps to analyze their wares in order to get an idea of the intellectual resources available to a community.

We have a long way to go toward understanding these important institutions, but there are excellent sources. Store ledgers and other business records may identify the titles in the store, as well as the suppliers and purchasers on account. Individual consumer names can be connected to specific titles, of course, and the overall consumption patterns of books and other printed materials can be analyzed. The ledgers may also indicate the markup or, in publishing parlance, the discounts on the books, along with other details of publisher-bookseller relations. Bookstore inventories are particularly useful, not only for seeing exactly what stock was on the floor at a specific moment, but also for reconstructing the proximity of different titles and, in general, the interior organization of the store's stock.[65]

Bookstore advertisements can also contain a wealth of information, including engravings or photographs of the interior, advertising copy indicating the bookseller's idea of what might help sell a particular book, the titles of books for sale, hours of store operations, and so forth. Not to be overlooked are the various publications of trade associations, like the American Booksellers Association, as well as the many how-to books published since the late nineteenth century. These can give some clues about the interior life and organization of bookstores, of so much value in the absence of first-person accounts from shoppers (a very rare occurrence in diaries and letters). Finally, to round out the picture of the bookstore, there are several autobiographies and biographies of specific booksellers.

b. Periodical Shops (Depots)

Somewhere in the shuffle of American book history one august institution became lost—the periodical depot. These shops, which apparently emerged in the 1840s, were not exactly like newsstands, though they did carry recent periodicals; they also sold books and pamphlets, as well as lozenges, patent medicines, and cigars. We can get a glimpse of one of these depots from a broadside issued by W. Little & Co., Boston, on the occasion of the funeral ceremonies for President Zachary Taylor in 1850. The sheet gives the parade order and order of services, but most of it is an advertisement for the store. As might be expected, the store offers the Boston daily and weekly newspapers, four papers from Philadelphia, twelve from New York, and sixteen from overseas, as well as magazines, listed under "Pictorial Monthlies," juvenile, medical, law, miscellaneous, and religious. What is surprising is the number of books and pamphlets, including plays, banknote lists, almanacs, phrenological and physiological works, and hundreds of novels. There are special notices for *The Fireman's Own Book* and sex advice manuals, too. To top it off, a block print depicts the lively interior of the store, populated by genteel men of all ages who are waited upon by clerks behind counters; newsboys in front hawk their wares, while a stiff-backed man with the word "police" in his hat brim patrols the scene. Apart from these types of advertisements (sometimes appearing on imprints themselves marketed by the shops), the only other access for book historians wishing to identify these institutions is through city directories.[66]

c. Book Agents/Peddlers

More familiar to book historians, but still largely underrated are the many traveling retailers who plied Americans with books. These were of several sorts, ranging from the colonial peddlers (often independent contractors) to agents garnering subscriptions. These travelers have quite some stories to tell, especially the women who set out in this line of work in the middle of the nineteenth century. More testament to their role in disseminating the printed word can be found in blads, or salesmen's dummies. These mock-ups of the books-to-be sometimes included a few sample pages with the edition binding wrapped around a slab of wood the projected size of the book. Manuscript itineraries or accounts of these travelers can tell book historians where publications were going and by whom they were being purchased.[67] Finally, some agents wrote reports to publishers, a few of which have survived; these provide some of the best information we have about the state of literary culture and taste in America's hinterlands.

d. Book Clubs

Book clubs have a distinguished history in America, stretching back at least as far as Benjamin Franklin's literary association, the Junto. The reason for the clubs remained the same throughout the nineteenth century as in Franklin's day: it was cheaper and more "beneficial" to pool books and subscriptions than to shoulder the cost alone.[68] Manuscript records of several of these reading clubs survive; they may give lists of members, minutes of meetings, records of materials read, reports of treasurers, and other details about these joint textual experiences, especially pertinent to the question of who read what when. One Worcester, Massachusetts, club focused on periodicals, according to its entry for 16 May 1849:"A meeting of friends, desirous of establishing a third club, for the reading of the leading periodicals &c. was held at the house of Jn°. C. Wyman."[69] By 1926 the term *book club* was appropriated by Harry Scherman as a marketing scheme, the Book-of-the-Month Club, which offered limited, "juried" selections to consumers via mail. Obviously, these types of clubs lacked the face-to-face interaction of the earlier organizations, but they performed a similar role of making the reader feel a part of a larger group.

e. General Merchandisers

Books and periodicals commonly have appeared in the stores of retailers that do not specialize in literature. Sometimes this was of necessity, since the local population may not have been large enough to support such specialized stores. In these cases general stores often took the bookstore's place. The many account books left by these stores are an excellent source for the book historian, for they not only allow for the connection between specific titles and names, but also give some indication of a family's other purchases. In fact, in towns with only one general store, the historian can calculate the percentage of the family's total expenditures given over to literature. The accounts can also be linked to nineteenth-century postmasters' records for the receipts of newspapers and magazines.[70] Books and periodicals could turn up in just about any retail establishment, however, and they were a feature of department stores right from their foundation in the mid-nineteenth century. By the twentieth century, books could also appear in supermarkets and in drugstores.

3 . AFTERMARKET

Not all books followed a predictable path from publisher to consumer, and the consumer may not have been the last stop in the line. One detour for books was to go upon the auction block; another was to go back upon the market.

a. Auctions

Book auctions, which had long been common in America as a way of selling off unwanted stock or property in probate, took on an additional function by the early nineteenth century: that of trade sales, held on specific days in the major publishing centers, where local buyers convened to sample the wares. Records of these events, while not abundant, do exist in manuscript.[71] More common are published advertisements or copies of the printed catalogs that were circulated before the auctions. The latter may give the author and title, state how many copies were placed on sale and in what covers, and list the asking price. A real boon for book historians are the numerous "priced" catalogs that can be found in research libraries. In these, someone has penciled in the actual winning bid; by comparing winning bids and asking prices, one can get a sense of what books were coveted by the auction goers and which were not.[72]

b. Used and Rare Books

Books purchased at auction or bought directly from publishers or consumers may fall into the hand of dealers specializing in used and rare books. The dealers are, in many ways, a breed apart from common booksellers, for they face the enormous challenge of satisfying a prospective purchaser's unusual penchant with an unusual book. Consequently, a hunter's instinct is not uncommon among this group, and their lives can make for good reading: many accounts of the most successful dealers are available. An important aspect of the trade is the ebb and flow of prices, which appear in published series as early as 1895; by quantify the price fluctuations, book historians can glimpse the unfolding development of the antiquarian book trade.

4. CONCLUSION

The dissemination routes discussed here are only some of the more common ways that books tumble into consumers' hands. Much work needs to be done, not only on specific channels of dissemination, but also on the relative economic and socio-cultural impact of different channels.

D. CONSUMERS

So far we have seen how the history of books can be approached through those who produced printed materials and those who disseminated them. But one other important group needs to be explored as a potential source of information—consumers. Historical consumers of print can help us chronicle how certain texts have been acquired, read, and passed down through generations. In this sense, consumers lend books their ultimate meaning, for books lie dormant in libraries, attics, or shops until someone uses them. As we will see, the category of "consumers" includes not only private individuals but also, in some cases, institutions such as libraries.

1. READERS

The ancient Greeks thought that inscribed words only came alive when people read them, preferably aloud. Readers literally gave "voice," hence vitality, to writings. To a great extent this notion still applies today—for example, when we appreciate the eloquence of a work written centuries ago, or when we are moved by verse composed in a distant time and feel that an author long dead still reaches us. As readers, therefore, we become as much a part of a book's history as the ink and paper that first brought it to life, when we pick it up, peruse it, think about it, sometimes are puzzled by it, discuss it with others, and remember it.

Discovering historical readers, especially "common readers"—the everyday people who by and large read most of the printed materials in existence—is not as easy as finding out about publishing processes or methods of distribution. Readers seldom left records of their reading experiences, for they did not believe them to be of historical significance. Even celebrated people, like canonical authors or prominent historical figures, often elude the investigator who longs to know what they thought about the books they owned. Historical audiences for particular books, especially those that were not best sellers, are just as difficult to determine. Yet many historians of the book have found ingenious ways of learning about readers from the past.

Precisely because of the scarcity of direct evidence about what historical readers thought as they read, some researchers focus upon "hypothetical readers." Simply put, hypothetical readers are conjectures based upon careful scrutiny of texts. The hypothetical reader has been called the "reader in the text," for this type of research involves a close reading of literature itself to find clues about who read it or was intended to read it, and how it was read. Books themselves contain hints about historical readers or audiences—for instance, in the subject matter of a book, its narrative, or in its price. For example, sentimental fiction, such as the nineteenth-century best seller *The Lamplighter,* is replete with domestic imagery and "woman's sphere" ideology, both of which upheld contemporary notions about Victorian family life and women's roles as wife and nurturer. The book, in its first edition, was also lengthy and bound in hard covers, making it relatively expensive. The "implied reader" of *The Lamplighter,* many researchers conclude, was probably a well-to-do woman.[73]

Studies of hypothetical readers, of course, are much more complex and subtle than the thumbnail sketch above implies. Such studies must take into account an inevitable fact of communication—misunderstanding. While authors may write with an "ideal reader" in mind (that is, one who understands precisely what a writer is trying to get across), there are in truth few such beings. Authors, try as they might, cannot always be interpreted as they intend. Some researchers take "misreading" into account as they ponder historical readers; like the game called telephone, one person's interpretation of a text, through the distortions of transmission, becomes a new, even creative, way of seeing it that is passed on to another. "Everything depends on who is doing the reading," one literary historian explains. For example, the Transcendentalist Margaret Fuller passed on her thoughts about Frederick Douglass's *Narrative* through her review in the *New York Daily Tribune*. Her own "misreading" had consequences, not necessarily negative, for the way we see Douglass's work today.[74] In a similar vein, literary specialists are always reinterpreting literature, showing us new ways of reading, say, Shakespeare or, at the other end of the spectrum, a dime novel. In fact, they themselves see their own work, the criticism of literature or the theorizing of interpretation (called *hermeneutics*), as subject to historical conditions that shape response. Just as we breathe life into a book when we read it—even if not with ideal comprehension—literary critics offer us their own less than ideal, but insightful and fresh readings of texts.

But some specialists feel that precisely because the reader is such an important part of the ongoing life of a book, texts are inseparable from readers. One went so far as to ask of his students: "Is there a text in this class?" People *are* the text; the best way to know a text is through actual "reader response." The understandings that readers bring to bear upon a book, regardless of what the author intended, ultimately determine how a book is received. There are as many ways to read a book as there are individual people; individuals, however, are not insulated from outside influences and instead form "interpretive communities" that contribute to the understanding of a book.[75]

Such regard for "reader response" has led historians of the book away from the text itself as the starting point for investigation. Why not go directly to the source—the "real reader"? Real readers, as opposed to hypothetical readers, are known, identifiable individuals who can tell us something about their encounters with books. Studying real readers is most easily done by interviewing living, breathing readers.[76] But how does one ask questions of the "dead informants"—the enormous chain of people who once cherished and pondered a particular piece of writing?[77]

a. Evidence in Books: Inscriptions, Marginalia, Book Plates, & Labels
Sometimes we are fortunate enough to hold in our hands the very book that others, perhaps great-grandparents or old friends, read many years ago, and we wonder: What did they think of this book when they first glanced at it? When did they buy it? Whom did they share it with? We may even see their handwritten notes (called *marginalia*) in the margins of the printed pages or their name carefully inscribed on the first page. Old Bibles may record genealogies or long lists of ancestors through which the volume was handed down. The personal jotting of names and thoughts provides evidence of historical ownership and readership. In an old book, one may sometimes find little scribbled notes throughout, such as "So true a tale" or "Paul Babcock His Book, 1805."[78] Some of the oldest books contain labels with a name to identify the owner; by the late eighteenth century these labels, often bearing intricate coats-of-arms, were being printed from copper plates and hence were called "book plates." Their use suggested a love of fine books, as well as gentlemanly refinement. Gift books, often ornately bound and illustrated annuals meant as holiday gifts or tokens of affection, occasionally have frontispieces printed for the purpose of recording the name of the giver and date presented. Such gift books were luxury items. At the other end of the spectrum of inscribed printed material is the lowly newspaper, sent cheaply as an economical way of keeping in touch.

Receiving a signed newspaper, or one with notes on stationery tucked away inside, reassured the recipient that the sender was alive and well or that he or she had safely reached a destination while traveling.

This type of evidence has its limitations. A name inscribed in a book may represent only one in a succession of owners and not all owners who signed books were their principal readers. Furthermore, people did not always wish to pause and write down notes to themselves as they read. Because writing in books could become a form of effacement, readers often limited the amount of marginalia. Book labels and gift-book frontispieces with blank lines reflect patterns of ownership mainly among wealthy folk, and even these links between names and books may not indicate actual readership. Even writing in newspapers sent in the mail presented problems, for if the postmaster happened to notice the "secret messages" within, he might charge the recipient for the cost of a letter; the threat of this discouraged the practice and severely limited the amount that could be written on these sheets.

b. Personal Papers

Apart from marginalia and inscriptions, there are other ways to understand what books people owned, what they thought about as they read them, and how they acquired and disposed of them. Personal papers, or collections containing a hodgepodge of diaries, letters, commonplace books, home library lists, and account books once belonging to members of a particular family, all contain more detailed evidence of readers' acquaintance with printed materials than can be gleaned from typical marginalia. Personal papers (also called family papers) may be published or, more commonly, in manuscript.

Collections of personal papers in manuscript can most often be located in large public and private repositories, state and local historical societies, and university libraries; but they also appear in some smaller public libraries, in churches or synagogues, and in a few private schools. Many archives publish catalogs of their family papers collections or list their holdings on-line.[79] If you have a general idea of the family or time frame that interests you, writing a letter of inquiry to the librarian or archivist of the repository will facilitate your research. Be advised that some papers remain in the hands of the families themselves, in which case you may have more difficulty in gaining access. Further, it is often necessary to obtain permission to use some collections, especially those of people still living or recently deceased, even if the papers have been deposited in archives. Personal papers may be published as books, as articles in scholarly periodicals, or on microfilm. Be aware that editors of published personal papers sometimes selectively edit out the very material of interest to historians of reading. Book titles, unfortunately, are often the first things to go. Although many collections of personal or family papers exist, they have by and large remained untapped as valuable sources for the study of reading.

i. Diaries. Family papers collections usually contain diaries and journals, which can be surprisingly rich sources for understanding the consumption of books. The term *diary* is often limited to material "written for personal reasons," while *journal* is applied to material "kept as part of a job" and, therefore, practical or utilitarian; nonetheless, archivists often use the two terms interchangeably. Some "literary journals" contain regular, often daily, records of book titles, the time of day the book was read, and whether it was read aloud or silently. Diaries may reveal where books were read: outdoors, in the attic, on the sofa, in the parlor, while alone, or in the company of others. Diarists often confided their thoughts about the books they read or the role books played in their acquisition of knowledge. There is no way of predicting exactly who kept literary diaries, and most archives do not list them under subject headings such as "reading," but the chances are greatest among white, middle-class, urban or suburban women or men who were not immersed in business (that is, retirees or students). But certainly literate people of all eras, ages, income levels, ethnicities, and religions kept diaries, and most diaries, except those compiled strictly for business purposes or visiting, will reward attentive searching for entries that in some way relate to getting and reading books. Sometimes one gets lucky and finds, tucked in the back pages of a diary or interspersed between entries, a "list of books I have read."[80]

ii. Family correspondence. Correspondence contains information similar to diaries, but letters often have more detailed responses to books, for sharing thoughts on reading was one way to keep communication alive, even at a distance, in earlier times. The exchange of thoughts on reading enlivens many a letter; for men and women contemplating marriage, books could even become "courting devices," as the couple pondered their compatibility through their responses to texts.[81] Less romantic letters might contain a thank-you for literary gifts or promises to exchange printed matter. Correspondents might tuck a newspaper clipping in an envelope as a way of sharing reading material. Letters, furthermore, give essential information not found in impersonal sources like advertisements, such as the valuation of books as consumer items within an expanding "world of goods."[82]

iii. Autobiographies. One kind of personal account that is rich in references to book consumption is the personal narrative, memoir, or autobiography. This type of record often reveals the author's relationship to books and the important role that study and reading played in his or her life trajectory. However, autobiographies and memoirs must be used with care. They are the product of both human creativity and memory; as such, they are both literary and historical. As historical documents, they are prone to human error: faulty recall, embellishment, self-censorship. As generally public forms, they are also subject to intervention, such as the mistakes of an amanuensis, the selectivity of an oral historian, the editing of the publisher, and the demands of the reading audience. But precisely because they were written with the public in mind, several autobiographies appear in published form, making them easily accessible. More important, autobiographies sometimes remain the only firsthand accounts of people who did not leave many other personal records for certain time periods—namely, Native Americans, African Americans, and immigrants.

In the case of many persons of African descent living under slavery between 1760 and 1865, a primary forum for recording their experiences with literacy was the "slave narrative," or "the written and dictated testimonies of the enslavement of black human beings."[83] Often punished for learning to read and write, slaves nonetheless struggled to become literate. In slave narratives the conditions surrounding literacy acquisition are almost always highlighted. Apart from containing vibrant accounts of the learning process, narratives use the language of the Bible and other religious texts, as well as abolitionist newspapers, and may refer to oral recitations, or "talking books," among other things relevant to reading.[84]

iv. Personal financial accounts. One of the best places to look for direct evidence of books as consumer items is in personal accounts. Account books of expenses often list titles of books, the days they were purchased, and the cost of the item. It is often difficult to determine for whom the book was purchased, but sometimes the account keeper jotted down a specific name. Personal account books also allow the investigator to determine what percentage of family expenditure was allotted to books and how books compared in price to other items of practical necessity, such as foods and fabrics. Account books may not be complete records of all purchases, however, and so must be used with caution when determining aggregate expenses.

v. Commonplace books and scrapbooks. Among collections of personal papers that contain diaries, letters, and account books, one may also find scrapbooks and commonplace books—rich, if frustrating, sources of information on reading. Although commonplace books generally include transcribed excerpts from literature, while scrapbooks are usually filled with clippings from printed sources, the two types of books seldom appear as entirely distinct in the age of print through the end of the nineteenth century, by which time the commonplace book was "well nigh gone."[85] Before the invention of printing, the commonplace book served to preserve passages from manuscripts that one might see only once in a lifetime. But even after printing appeared, people would copy enjoyable parts of a borrowed book so that they could recall the reading experience after the book had been returned; or they would paste in favorite news items or poetry from ephemeral sources in order to savor them in the future, often into old age. The practice also seems to have been a way mentally to organize, extract, and then arrange by topic gleanings from a vast field of print. The most difficult part of using both commonplace books and scrapbooks is in ascertaining the source of the literary fragment, for often people recorded parts of literature without giving credit to the author or edition, or they failed to disclose the newspaper from which a piece was clipped. As disappointing is the persistent failure on the part of the compiler to date the items in these books, which often evolved over decades of a lifetime. Some help both in identifying quotations and, to a lesser extent, in dating them can be found in a series of on-line databases, published by Chadwyck-Healey, Ltd., devoted to reproducing the full texts of a vast array of English and American belles-lettres (mostly poetry and drama). Database users can search the entire corpus for the occurrence of a particular combination of words in order to identify the source and its date of publication.

Apart from suggesting reading preferences, commonplace books and scrapbooks reveal states of mind as constructed through reading. For example, in colonial Virginia, William Byrd II revealed in his commonplace book "a concern with controlling his emotions." Commonplace books of prominent people like Byrd or the young Thomas Jefferson (he found release in poetry while studying law, and his extracts persistently touch upon the theme of death) are the most likely to have been studied. The average person's mental universe awaits more research through this intriguing source.[86]

vi. Personal library lists. While the significance of entries in commonplace books often remains elusive, the books that people had in their personal libraries are forthright statements of book ownership—and, some say, consequently of reading. The libraries of wealthy people, such as William Byrd II, whose vast collection was catalogued shortly after his death, have been subject to scholarly investigation. Prominent authors, however, have received the most attention. For some, like Ralph Waldo Emerson, their collections remained relatively intact and were deposited in historical societies or other repositories. Lists of books can fairly easily be recorded and cataloged in printed form for others to study. Some scholars will go to great lengths to reconstruct what sat upon authors' bookshelves, by tracking down inscribed copies of books that have been scattered about. Not satisfied with merely knowing and listing what a writer owned, researchers also look at auction catalogs or library charge records to see what he or she borrowed and placed, temporarily at least, among his or her personal collection.[87] Many researchers begin with only lists, but in calling upon other materials, such as notes left inside books, diary entries, and marginalia, they create broader interpretive studies that illuminate the artistic creations of authors or the lifestyles of "gentlemen" through their reading habits and preferences. For book historians who are not versed in bibliography, these lists compiled by others may form the basis for such interpretation. There are many such lists, widely available in printed form, but as yet no bibliographical guide to them has been published.

c. Institutionally Generated Evidence of Reading

There are many ways to understand the history of reading that augment or even circumvent the study of personal papers. The documents of institutions are another body of information that researchers have used with great success. Legal or government documents, such as probate inventories or postmaster's records, are one subset of this type of source. Other institutional records, such as a library's charge lists, book subscription lists, a publisher's book auctions, or sponsored surveys of reading habits, are another. Documents like these are relatively easy to locate in public libraries or a local historical society, and unlike most personal papers, they quite often appear on microfilm or in printed form. Like personal papers, however, they must be used with discretion; carefully handled and creatively mined for information, printed documents can yield valuable clues about historical readers.

i. Probate inventories and other public documents. Legal and government documents, such as census data, court records, and especially probate records (containing wills and those tedious inventories of a deceased person's property or estate recorded for judicial action), seem unlikely sources for the study of reading. They are surprisingly fertile, however, especially for determining literacy. (*Literacy,* although difficult to define, especially within a historical context, typically means the ability to read or both to read *and* write.)

Wills and other signed documents, such as deeds, marriage records, or petitions, may reveal that the signer was literate. Although there is much debate over the validity of signatures as sure signs of literacy (sometimes a "signature" is merely an "X" mark on a document), signatures serve as a starting point for estimating the degree to which certain colonial and early American populations were part of the general reading public. It is much easier to estimate literacy in the modern era, but although information is readily accessible, it cannot always be accepted unquestioningly. For the eighteenth and early nineteenth centuries there are ample court records with signatures, but from the mid-nineteenth century on, the most commonly used indicator, at least of self-reported literacy, is census data: beginning in 1840 the census included a question about literacy. But researchers have refined their methods of inquiry to investigate more complex issues, such as the degree of literacy attained. To this end, they have designed a variety of studies that use, augment, or bypass the census; these include "then-and-now" studies comparing reading ability over time, standardized achievement tests and other measures of education attainment, functional literacy tests, and assessments of job performance.

According to one survey of nineteenth-century literacy:

> The historical study of such a fundamental process as the
> development of literacy in the making of modern civiliza-
> tions is still in its infancy—a result, in part, of the traditional
> reluctance of historians to accept and apply the quantitative
> techniques capable of generating a comprehensive selecting
> and weighing of those factors which determine the rise
> and perpetuation of literacy.[88]

Most historians of the book are not content with merely determining literacy rates. Carl Kaestle remarks that "a broad history
of literacy must look beyond the labels of 'illiterate' and 'literate'
to study the functions of reading."[89] Researchers make use of
relevant data to frame larger questions and construct theories
about the correlation of literacy with such factors as wealth and
occupation or high population density. They study its relationship to reading publics and consider how the "ideology" of literacy was spread through schools or by the proliferation of
inexpensive printed materials, like newspapers. These researchers determine the meaning of literacy for distinct populations or its long-term effects upon society in general. For
example, how high a level of literacy is necessary for a person to
enjoy reading? In studying colonial women's literacy, E. Jennifer
Monaghan notes, "we should not underestimate the pleasure
that even a limited reading ability can bring."[90] Researchers
ponder the paradox that for much of American history, the in-
ability to read has made people dependent, but has not necessarily marginalized them, for illiterate people often took an
active role in community or civic duty. Nor has illiteracy pre-
cluded learning from oral reading. Yet illiteracy is and has always
been seen as a serious liability—especially in its pernicious
effects upon racial and ethnic minorities and low-income
groups; consequently, researchers wish to understand its causes.
In this era of electronic media that invites visual, but nontextual,
forms of learning, such as television viewing or even Internet
surfing, is the ability of Americans to read, or to find pleasure in
the act, diminishing along with the ability to think and act criti-

cally? Daniel Boorstin reminds us that "our democracy is based on books and reading."[91]

Many book historians who use probate records go beyond locating signatures to studying the content of inventories. Upon the death of the head of a household, inventory takers were—and still are at times—called in to assess the value of the deceased person's property. Quite often they listed valuable books among other items left in a person's estate. Although the books listed have long since disappeared, their titles are sometimes immortalized in probate inventories. The "Large Family Bible" of Edward Ambush, an African American of Boston, "even if physically lost to posterity, manages to project a strong presence that eloquently reveals preferences."[92] Since the earliest European settlement of America, large numbers of inventories have been taken almost every year in just about every county. Because they represent so many people's possessions over such a long period of time, historians have used them to discover large-scale changes in reading preferences. Assuming that if a person owned a book, he or she read it, researchers have compiled lists of the most favored titles or genres read among certain historical segments of the population. Some investigators have even tried to find out just when in the past reading became so important as an activity, even a "necessity of life," for average rural people.[93] Using probate inventories, one can quickly accumulate large numbers of titles even if one "samples" (looking for example, at the decadal years, 1800, 1810, 1820, and so forth, in only a few counties in one state). Probates, therefore, lend themselves easily to quantification and correlations—those possible links between at least two factors, such as wealth (as deduced from the other property listed in the inventory) and size of a family library.[94]

Although probate records are intriguing sources, they have their limitations, especially when used without support from the other types of sources discussed above. These records do not give much insight into individuals' unique relationship to reading: what they thought of the books they read, when they read the books they owned, or even if they read them at all. How often do we today buy, with good intentions, books we will never read? But despite these and other limitations, inventories deserve to play a larger role in studying reading history than they have in the past.

ii. Book-trade subscription lists. Other underutilized sources for determining book ownership among individuals or groups are book-trade subscription lists. Subscription lists can be used to plot the geographical boundaries of readers of particular books or to understand the literary tastes of individuals or occupational groups. They are found sometimes at the beginning or end pages of the books sold by subscription (especially in the eighteenth century, when dealing with American publications); there are also some manuscript lists of subscribers, but these are more rarely found.

The Book Subscription Lists Project (reorganized in 1975 as the Project for Historical Biobibliography), begun in 1971 at the University of Newcastle upon Tyne, England, has compiled thousands of books published between 1617 and the present that contain subscription lists. In 1973 the project began to computerize its information with files containing the subscribers' name, class status, and address, and the title of the book purchased. Such data can yield, for example, lists of titles with more than a thousand subscribers, the names and occupations of subscribers to a particular edition, and books subscribed to by particular individuals. The project's director, P. J. Wallis, describes subscription lists as "largely unused but important historical record[s] of significance in every aspect of British social history."[95]

This massive effort has not been duplicated for American books; in fact, little compilation, let alone analysis, has been done at all. Most studies of book subscription in America approach the topic from the angle of the publishing industry and not the reader. Yet subscription lists, if one can locate them, contain information of great potential use. Certainly the practice of obtaining subscribers for books continued into the late nineteenth century and beyond. "Be very particular to write yourself the *occupation,* and the residence of the subscriber, and also the *Style of Binding* he is to have," one publisher advised his agents in 1874. Janice Radway's recent work on the Book-of-the-Month Club is valuable for understanding twentieth-century subscribers and contemporary "middle brow" literary culture as well.[96]

iii. Photographs and drawings. Visual material is a neglected source for the study of readers, especially in the nineteenth century, when photographic shots of people reading were common (probably because of slow camera shutter speeds). This type of material must be used cautiously, however, for it is influenced by an ideology of genteel literary consumption that may not represent life as actually lived. For example, some people known to have been illiterate were photographed with book in hand. More reliable are visual images that record evidence of print culture by accident. For example, Thomas C. Leonard examined Farm Security Administration photographs taken of sharecroppers' homes for the appearance of clippings of magazine and newspapers illustrations and advertisements hung upon their walls.[97]

iv. Surveys and scientific studies. At the end of the nineteenth century American industrialists began to turn to the social sciences to help them understand their prospective markets in order to serve their customers better and to generate more sales in so doing. Faith was high that by relying upon social science expertise, management would at long last solve the persistent problem of overproduction, which in the book trade meant producing too many titles that too few people wished to read. As a result, publishers embarked on a quest for "the reader" (by which they usually meant the purchaser of books or periodicals). The results, though often flawed by faulty assumptions and questionable methodologies, are useful to book historians, because publishers throughout the twentieth century have based their decisions upon those findings.

v. Library charge records. A goldmine for book historians exists in the various manuscript charge records of social and public libraries. These records can be organized either in "daybook" fashion, in which charges are registered sequentially, or by patron. In either case, the records contain the name of the patron, a short title of the volume borrowed, the date borrowed, and the date returned. Since this is a mountain of information, it should be entered into a computer database that permits the researcher to sort and quantify the data on all four fields: patron, title, date charged, date returned. It is then possible to analyze the data and find correlations. For example, one might assemble the full borrowing list of a family and trace evolving patterns of interest or situate certain types of works or works by specific authors within the greater whole of materials borrowed.

Another approach to library charges entails using census manuscript rolls (discussed earlier) to find out the age, residence, profession, and household composition of those patrons who charged out books. The first task is to identify the head of the household in which a patron lived—easier for men than for women. After census records, one may refer to local tax rolls; these give information on people rich enough to pay a certain amount of taxes. This information may permit the correlation of wealth with specific reading patterns. In short, charge records offer book historians an unusually systematic set of data to understand overall literary patterns.

2. INSTITUTIONAL CONSUMERS

Throughout U.S. history, books and periodicals have been purchased not only by individuals but also by institutions. Institutional purchases usually serve a specific goal, such as the development of a collection or an internal body of knowledge. It may, of course, still be an individual who is given the authority to make purchases, but the decisions are generally made in light of the objectives of the institution. Further, the institutions may go on to create borrowing or browsing opportunities for individual readers.

a. Libraries
Among the steadiest and most voracious institutional consumers are the many American libraries, private and public.

Indeed, the history of libraries is a vibrant field of study, with its own scholarly journal (*Libraries & Culture*), professional organization (the American Library Association's Library History Roundtable), graduate-school concentration, bibliographies, and multi-volume collaborative overview in the works.[98] So there is a strong scholarly tradition upon which book historians working in other disciplines may rely.

Many sources and methods are available to book historians wishing to explore libraries as institutional consumers of books. Because librarians early on kept archives of organizational activities, purchase records sometimes can be found which may give direct evidence of who made the decision to purchase, when, and from whom. Short of such direct evidence, library catalogs, both published and in manuscript, can be systematically analyzed for such factors as the relative percentages of varying genres appearing in them. Robert B. Winans analyzed most of the surviving eighteenth-century catalogs to conclude that British sentimental fiction was much more prevalent in America than had previously been thought. Not every library published a catalog, and not every published catalog survives; short of that, advertisements in periodicals or in handbills can be useful, and in the case of commercial circulating libraries, these may be all that is left to testify to their holdings. Sometimes annual reports of libraries list books added to the collection in the previous year, and they usually give general patron and financial data that may be useful for book historians.[99] Historians who wish to reconstruct past library practices and internal organization may find that more promising sources—if approached with a critical eye—are manuals and professional journals. The library profession's commitment to serving its public has also led to several surveys and scientific studies of library patrons' behavior.

b. Schools

Besides libraries, both public and private schools have been and continue to be major consumers of printed materials. Of course, many schools maintain their own libraries, but they usually spend much more money in textbook adoptions. Evidence of such adoptions through much of U.S. history is elusive; the best starting point is probably the annual reports of schools and school systems, but these are neither well indexed nor widely available. Accounts of a school's curriculum (often issued by private schools as part of their advertisements) may contain either direct or indirect evidence of printed materials used, and there are miscellaneous addresses by school officials as well as firsthand accounts from teachers and students to add to the book historian's toolkit.

c. Other

Three other institutional purchasers of books and periodicals must be mentioned. First, religious organizations of varying sorts have used print material in generally two fundamental ways: for external distribution to laypeople and for internal consumption by clergy. Both types of use date back to the earliest Puritan settlers in New England and parish libraries in the South, but by the early nineteenth century some large religious organizations were developing such systematic distribution of print materials that they resembled the information management systems of late nineteenth-century corporations.[100] Second, businesses, especially large, modern corporations, frequently maintain their own in-house specialized libraries or purchase professional materials for their employees; for example, over the past two decades there has been an explosion of computer manuals. Although this is a little-studied phenomenon, book historians can gain some insight from the listings in the American Library Association's annual directory. One way to learn more about the internal use of published sources by technology-intensive corporations over the past few decades is through the field of information science, which grew up to help manage the flood of documents these corporations encounter as they attempt to make informed decisions based on the latest technical advances. Third, government at all levels—itself a large producer of print materials—also consumes print matter from nongovernmental sources. Somewhere between the second and the third types of institutional purchasers are the many private-interest lobbying groups (some of which have their own think tanks) that compete to shape public policy; these also purchase great numbers of books and periodicals in the subject areas with which they are concerned.

3. THE BOOK TRADE ITSELF

Book and periodical production is somewhat self-reflexive, since the rest of the trade pays close attention to what is tumbling off the press. A relatively small proportion of an edition goes no further than the trade itself and is often distributed free, but it may have a disproportionate impact on current sales of the title and subsequent publications of a similar nature. Review media are the most common destination for these free copies, but there are also digests. Publishing firms may also purchase a range of titles to assist in editorial work or to keep an eye on the competition. In the nineteenth century, periodical publishers routinely exchanged copies with other, similar publications, usually to facilitate the "borrowing" of copy, while crediting the source. An illegal or ethically dubious form of internal consumption is that of piracy/plagiarism, in which the literary property is "consumed" for purposes of appropriation. Books can beget other books legitimately if the original source is properly quoted and cited, so authors themselves often consult many books as they prepare their manuscripts. This more conventional influence on authorship and publishing leaves traces of what modern literary critics call "intertextuality"—clear lines of discursive descent from one text to another. The range of previous works confronting authors can be awe-inspiring, so much so that one literary critic, Harold Bloom, speaks of "the anxiety of influence" as an important, perhaps the defining, psychological challenge of authorship.[101]

III. Conclusion:
The Future of Book History

WE HAVE set out some of the rich possibilities for book historians today and have alluded to prior notable work. It should be clear that book history is indeed complex and varied—and that there is much room for people to make further contributions to the field. Even an awareness of the important role print culture has played in American life helps to sustain it in the face of threats from new technologies, poor adult reading comprehension, and, perhaps above all, a pervasive sociocultural malaise, even apathy, over the fate of learning.

In spite of cultural observers who bemoan the state of the book today, the future for book history research looks bright, indeed. The Society for the History of Authorship, Reading, and Publishing (SHARP) provides a forum through which people from various disciplines can exchange ideas; there are also several local interdisciplinary research centers of scholars working on book history. Scholarly series in book history have been founded by Pennsylvania State University Press, the University of Massachusetts Press, and Cambridge University Press.

This institutional development promises some new directions for book history. The interdisciplinary nature of the development has created a space for discussion among groups that previously had little mutual contact: bibliographers and historians, sociologists and literary scholars, and so forth. These discussions hold out the hope that book history may be approaching a synthesis of its varied and often fragmented specializations. At the same time, as book historians ask questions about their field, they are uncovering huge gaps in the scholarship that may frustrate premature efforts at synthesis. Interdisciplinary discussion has also made book historians more methodologically sophisticated and creative.

Perhaps the most important new direction has been the rise of the history of reading, for long the poor stepsister of the author/publisher complex. Reading represents more than a new topic, however. It promises a firmer connection to cultural history than was possible through the study of authorship or publishing, for both of those approaches had to rely heavily upon some theoretical structure to attain any sense of larger significance. After all, no one doubts that readers are cultural representatives, at least of their own culture, but it is quite another matter to argue that publishers or authors speak for their readers, in the absence of corroborating testimony from readers.

New sources are helping to develop the history of the book, too. One neglected "new" source—long available to librarians but only recently to others—is the electronic library catalog. Keyword searches using faster computers and modems have dramatically increased the pace of bibliographical identification—a key component of book history. These catalogs also help book historians by facilitating the recovery of formerly obscure sources of book history—particularly trade materials, but also, increasingly, manuscripts originating from all points in the circuit of production, dissemination, and consumption. Ironically, as book historians have become more aware of the mediations of print, manuscript evidence has been gaining new value—not just because it is not as heavily mediated, but also because it provides a different perspective. Other new sources are scanned books and periodical files, which can be analyzed quantitatively or graphically.

Along with these new sources, new techniques are emerging for book historians, too. Developments are occurring in three general areas: microcomputer-based quantification; optical character recognition, which opens the possibility that data will no longer have to be keyed in, but only proofread and corrected; and record linkage between data sets made of authors, producers, disseminators, and consumers.

Another new technique borrows from the old one of intensive textual analysis. The New Critics made such analysis of important texts their strong point, while they neglected and even disparaged historicist studies of authorship and production that remain the focus of much work of book historians today. But some book historians are redeploying intensive textual analysis away from printed texts themselves and applying it instead to the texts that readers have left—for example, in the form of letters and diaries—about the printed materials they encountered. After all, this is one good approach to exploring the history of meaning that we mentioned at the outset.

Once it is clear that book history contributes to the history of meaning (a greater project being pursued by cultural historians all over the world), its role in the electronic information age becomes clearer as well. For the sociocultural mediations of print resemble in many ways those of other media. But with book history we have great longitudinal advantage, for the study stretches back to the mid-fifteenth century. In that vast pageant of history, the book has played many roles indeed—a reminder to prophets and critics who view mediating technologies in a deterministic fashion, as heralding either an electronic utopia or dystopia.

Some Important Periodicals
for Book Historians

AB Bookman's Weekly (1967–)

Advertising Age (1930–)

American Journalism (1983–)

American Literature (1929–)

American Model Printer (1879–82)

American Periodicals (1991–)

American Pressman (1890–1968)

American Printing History Association Newsletter (1974–)

Antiquarian Bookman (1948–67)

Bibliographical Society, Transactions (1892–1920)

Bibliographical Society of America, Papers (1904–)

Bibliographical Society of Canada, Papers (1962–)

Bibliographie der Buch- und Bibliothekgeschichte (1982–)

Bibliography Newsletter (1973–80)

Biblion: The Bulletin of the New York Public Library (1992–)

Book Club of California Quarterly News Letter (1933–)

Book Collector (1952–61)

Book History (1998–)

Bookplate Journal (1983–90)

Book Research Quarterly (1985–91)

Books at Brown (1938–)

Books at Iowa (1964–96)

Book Trade History Group Newsletter (1986–)

Bookways (1991–)

British Library Journal (1975–)

Bull and Branch (1991–)

Bulletin du Bibliophile (1834–1962)

Bulletin of Research in the Humanities (1978–87)

Bulletin of the New York Public Library (1897–1977)

Choice (1964–)

Collectible Newspapers (1984–)

The Craftsman (1967–)

Daguerrian Annual (1990–)

Dime Novel Round-Up (1931–)

Early American Literature (1966–)

Editor & Publisher (1901–)

Emerson Society Quarterly (ESQ) (1955–)

Ephemera Journal (1987–)

Fourth Estate (1894–1927)

Gazette of the Grolier Club (1921–48; 1966–)

Graphic Arts Monthly (1929–)

Guild of Book Workers Journal (1962–)

Guild Reporter (1933–)

Gutenberg-Jahrbuch (1926–)

Hand Papermaking (1986–)

Harvard Library Bulletin (1947–)

History of Reading News (1976–)

Huntington Library Quarterly (1937–)

Imprint (1976–)

Ink & Gall (1987–)

Inland Printer (later *American Printer*) (1883–)

Journalism and Mass Communication Quarterly (1995–)

Journalism History (1974–)

Journalism Quarterly (1928–95)

Journalist (1884–1907)

Journal of Library History (title varies) (1966–87)

Journal of the Printing Historical Society (1965–)

Libraries & Culture (1988–)

Library Quarterly (1931–)

Map Collector (1977–96)

Miniature Book News (1965–73; 1978–87)

New Bookbinder (1981–)

New England Book and Text Studies (1994–)

Newspaperdom (1892–1924)

Numismatic Literature (1947–)

Old Print Shop Portfolio (1941–c. 1977)

The Paper Maker (later *Paper*) (1932–70)

Print Collector's Newsletter (1970–96)

Printer's Ink (later *Marketing/Communications*) (1888–1967)

Printing History (1979–)

Print Quarterly (1984–)

Proof-Sheet (1867–82)

P. S. A Quarterly Journal of Postal History (1977–93)

Publishers' Auxiliary (1865–)

Publishing History (1977–)

Publishing Research Quarterly (1991–)

Rare Books and Manuscript Librarianship (1986–)

Resources for American Literary Study (1971–)

Scholarly Publishing, Journal (1969–)

SHARP News (1991–)

Studies in Bibliography (1949–)

Studies in Bibliography and Booklore (1953–)

Studies in the American Renaissance (1977–95)

Typographical Journal (1889–)

Wolfenbütteler Bibliotheks-Informationen (1976–)

Notes

1. Christopher T. Keith, Diaries, 1854–71, vol. 1, entry for 16 February 1858, Miscellaneous Manuscript Collection, Rhode Island Historical Society, Providence. These quotations are discussed in Ronald J. Zboray and Mary Saracino Zboray, "Transcendentalism in Print: Production, Dissemination, and Common Reception," in *Transient and Permanent: The Transcendentalist Movement and Its Contexts,* ed. Charles Capper and Conrad Edick Wright (Boston: Massachusetts Historical Society, 1999), 310–81.

2. Harriet Low, Diary, entry for 13 April 1831, transcript, Peabody Essex Museum, Salem, Mass.; original in the Library of Congress, Washington, D.C.

3. Of course, the term *history of the book* is in reality a shorthand for a much broader array of printed materials that includes, for example, newspapers, magazines, handbills, broadsides—all that can be placed under the rubric of "imprints."

4. Richard W. Clement, *The Book in America: With Images from the Library of Congress* (Golden, Colo.: Fulcrum Publishing, 1996), 140.

5. John Y. Cole, "Storehouses and Workshops: American Libraries and the Uses of Knowledge," in *The Organization of Knowledge in Modern America, 1860–1920,* ed. Alexandra Oleson and John Voss (Baltimore: Johns Hopkins University Press, 1979).

6. The literature on the new historicism is enormous; for an introduction, see H. Aram Veeser, ed., *The New Historicism* (New York: Routledge, 1989).

7. Stephen Greenblatt, *Renaissance Self-Fashioning from More to Shakespeare* (Chicago: University of Chicago Press, 1980).

8. William H. Bouwsma, "Intellectual History in the 1980s: From History of Ideas to History of Meaning," *Journal of Interdisciplinary History* 12 (Autumn 1981): 279–91; John E. Toews, "Intellectual History after the Linguistic Turn: The Autonomy of Meaning and the Irreducibility of Experience," *American Historical Review* 92 (October 1987): 879–907.

9. William Charvat, *Literary Publishing in America, 1790–1850* (1959; reprint, Amherst: University of Massachusetts Press, 1993), 7.

10. The themes were sounded by David D. Hall, "Prospectus: A History of the Book in American Culture," supplement to *The Book:*

Newsletter of the Program in the History of the Book in American Culture 16 (1988): 1–4. The evolution of the phrase can be seen in Hall, *Cultures of Print: Essays in the History of the Book* (Amherst: University of Massachusetts Press, 1996).

11. The Library of Congress on-line catalog for pre-1956 imprints (it actually goes to 1968 for English-language material and to 1970 for material in other languages), PREMARC, consists of approximately 4.8 million records. Although this covers only LC materials, while the *NUC* contains contributing library entries, the on-line catalog is relatively complete. Still, *NUC* and other LC printed catalogs are more so. The on-line records have been electronically converted from the LC shelflist and hence do not have the detail of full, standard modern cataloging under the MARC (*MA*chine-*R*eadable *C*ataloging) format, which is available at other large institutions. However, 1.3 million of the original scanty on-line records are scheduled to be replaced shortly with full-blown OCLC records. We thank Kay D. Guiles, cataloging policy specialist, Library of Congress, for this information.

12. Every year sees new electronic catalog resources; for example, OCLC's WorldCat is available at some university libraries and permits single searches through a large universe of institutions. Detailed searching and data retrieval are also offered through some older networks, like OCLC and RLIN, though access to the resources is usually restricted.

13. The *English Short-Title Catalogue,* available on-line, gives broad coverage (from the beginnings of printing to 1800), but because of the nature of the work does not provide much description of individual items.

14. The birth of printing-trade papers is covered in Ronald J. Zboray, *A Fictive People: Antebellum Economic Development and the American Reading Public* (New York: Oxford University Press, 1993), 18–24. These papers descend in a more or less direct line from *Norton's Literary Gazette and Publishers' Circular* (1851) to today's *Publishers Weekly.* Publishing firms are traditionally called "houses" because of their artisanal roots in early printing shops with living quarters for masters, apprentices, and sometimes journeymen. See Ronald J. Zboray, "Books," in *Handbook on Mass Media in the United States: The Industry and Its Audiences,* ed. Erwin K. Thomas and Brown H. Carpenter (Westport, Conn.: Greenwood Press, 1994), 19–37.

15. For this type of analysis, see Ronald J. Zboray and Mary Saracino Zboray, "The Boston Book Trades, 1789–1850: A Statistical and Geographical Analysis," in *Entrepreneurs: The Boston Business Community, 1700–1850,* ed. Conrad Edick Wright and Katheryn P. Viens (Boston: Massachusetts Historical Society, 1997), 210–67.

16. Every Boston city directory before 1851 was looked at in the preparation of Zboray and Zboray, "The Boston Book Trades, 1789–1850."

17. D'Alté A. Welch, *A Bibliography of American Children's Books Printed prior to 1821* (1963; reprint, Worcester, Mass.: American Antiquarian Society, 1972). The American Antiquarian Society's on-line catalog now augments Welch and extends bibliographical control, based on the society's large holdings, until 1876 (this includes Canadian children's books as well).

18. For an excellent demonstration of the uses of history-of-the-book methodology for studying science, one that underscores the generalizations made here, see Nathan Reingold, "Definitions and Speculations: The Professionalization of Science in America in the Nineteenth Century," in *The Pursuit of Knowledge in the Early American Republic: American Scientific and Learned Societies from Colonial Times to the Civil War,* ed. Alexandra Oleson and Sanborn C. Brown (Baltimore: Johns Hopkins University Press, 1976), 33–69.

19. Hall, *Cultures of Print,* 5.

20. The following tripartite division of the history of the book into production, dissemination, and consumption (or reception) is discussed in Zboray and Zboray, "Transcendentalism in Print."

21. Lawrence Buell, *New England Literary Culture: From Revolution through Renaissance* (Cambridge: Cambridge University Press, 1986), notes for antebellum authorship "three levels of literary activity: the socioeconomic level of literary publishing, the ideological level of literary values, and the aesthetic level of the literary artifacts themselves" (56).

22. Some scholars have explored the concept of authorship as applied to "manuscript" publications, circulated in either single or multiple copies. See, for example, David S. Shields, *Civil Tongues and Polite Letters in British America* (Chapel Hill: University of North Carolina Press, 1997). Early printed books in many ways simply picked up where the products of the medieval and Renaissance scriptoria (that is, "factories" of scribes who reproduced manuscript texts) left off. But as printing developed new forms, such as the newspaper, even handwritten documents occasionally were structured by conventions derived from print culture. Examples include the many manuscript amateur newspapers emerging from schools and lyceums in the nineteenth century.

23. William Charvat, *The Profession of Authorship in America, 1800–1870: The Papers of William Charvat,* ed. Matthew J. Bruccoli (Columbus: Ohio State University Press, 1968), 168. Michael Davitt Bell's essay "Conditions of Literary Vocation," which builds upon Charvat's work, is the best place to start for a general overview; see *The Cambridge History of American*

Literature, vol. 2, *Prose Writing, 1820–1865,* ed. Sacvan Bercovitch (Cambridge: Cambridge University Press, 1995), 9–124.

24. Charvat's "Longfellow's Income from His Writings, 1840–1852" (chap. 9 of *Profession of Authorship*) is especially helpful in highlighting some of the tools for studying authorship: Longfellow's account books, contracts, copyright documents, bills for stereotyping, and letters from publishers and editors to Longfellow. For more discussion on authors' dealings with publishers, see below.

25. Buell, *New England Literary Culture,* 382, 375–92 (appendix). His prosopography of 276 authors who reached "literary maturity between 1770 and 1865" is based upon biographical sketches from standard reference works.

26. Mary Kelley, *Private Woman, Public Stage: Literary Domesticity in Nineteenth-Century America* (New York: Oxford University Press, 1984).

27. Susan Coultrap-McQuin, *Doing Literary Business: American Women Writers in the Nineteenth Century* (Chapel Hill: University of North Carolina Press, 1990), especially chap. 5; Gail Hamilton [Mary Abigail Dodge], *A Battle of the Books, Recorded by an Unknown Writer for the Use of Authors and Publishers* (Cambridge, Mass.: Riverside Press, 1870).

28. On one of the earliest short-term professional novelists, see Steven Watts, *The Romance of Real Life: Charles Brockden Brown and the Origins of American Culture* (Baltimore: Johns Hopkins University Press, 1994).

29. The authorship of the individual papers has given rise to a lively debate. Some of the most useful work for book historians centers on computer analysis of style. See, for example, F. J. Tweedie, S. Singh, and D. I. Holmes, "Neural Network Applications in Stylometry: The Federalist Papers," *Computers and the Humanities* [Netherlands] 30 (1996): 1–10.

30. Jürgen Habermas formulated the idea of the public sphere almost forty years ago, and Michael Warner first articulated the impact of Habermas's public sphere for early American authorship—a position with which Grantland S. Rice takes issue.

31. Charvat, *Profession of Authorship,* 284. Charvat explores in three concluding chapters the effects that society, the reading public, and economics might have exerted upon authors.

32. Ezra Greenspan, *Walt Whitman and the American Reader* (Cambridge: Cambridge University Press, 1990), chooses one writer's biography to explore the relationship among democracy, culture, and authorship. Kenneth Dauber, *The Idea of Authorship in America: Democratic Poetics from Franklin to Melville* (Madison: University of Wisconsin Press, 1990), xvii.

33. Stephen Railton, *Authorship and Audience: Literary Performance in the American Renaissance* (Princeton, N.J.: Princeton University Press, 1991), 201. Railton follows Charvat's lead in *Profession of Authorship,* especially his

chapter 13, "Melville and the Common Reader," which calls upon the author's prefaces to his works and "autobiographical passages" in the novels (282n.5). William G. Rowland Jr., *Literature and the Marketplace: Romantic Writers and Their Audiences in Great Britain and the United States* (Lincoln: University of Nebraska Press, 1996), 1.

34. The oft-cited figures derive from Samuel G. Goodrich, *Recollections of a Lifetime; or, Men and Things I Have Seen,* 2 vols. (New York: Miller, Orton & Mulligan, 1856), 2:389.

35. It is important to point out that although Stowe's book may have arisen from local needs, as suggested by its initial serial appearance in a reform paper, it nevertheless ultimately had broad international appeal. Indeed, Richard Altick, in *The English Common Reader: A Social History of the Mass Reading Public, 1800–1900* (Chicago: University of Chicago Press, 1957), used the book to measure the widest extent of the British reading public.

36. Michael Anesko, *"Friction with the Market": Henry James and the Profession of Authorship* (New York: Oxford University Press, 1986), ix.

37. Christopher P. Wilson, *The Labor of Words: Literary Professionalism in the Progressive Era* (Athens: University of Georgia Press, 1985), 198–99. James L. West III disagrees with Wilson's view of the synchrony of authorial and greater middle-class professionalization, calling the laboring conditions of writers since 1900 "anachronistic" (*American Authors and the Literary Marketplace since 1900* [Philadelphia: University of Pennsylvania Press, 1988], 20).

38. Andrew Levy, *The Culture and Commerce of the American Short Story* (Cambridge: Cambridge University Press, 1993), chap. 4.

39. Ernest Hemingway, *Ernest Hemingway on Writing,* ed. Larry W. Phillips (New York: Scribner's, 1984). On the Victorian quality of his letters to his mother, see Ann Douglas, *Terrible Honesty: Mongrel Manhattan in the 1920s* (New York: Farrar, Straus & Giroux, 1995), 195–200.

40. Although much of our discussion of authorship has focused on fiction or bellettristic writers, many of the trends affect nonfiction writers, too.

41. Modern Language Association of America, Center for Scholarly Editions, *The Center for Scholarly Editions: An Introductory Statement* (New York: Modern Language Association of America, 1997).

42. The best historical overview of the role of the agent in American publishing can be found in West, *American Authors and the Literary Marketplace,* chap. 5.

43. Two relevant manuscript collections are those of Paul Revere Reynolds at Columbia University and Flora May Holly at the New York Public Library.

44. Lewis A. Coser, Charles Kadushin, and Walter W. Powell, *Books: The*

Culture and Commerce of Publishing (New York: Basic Books, 1982). For a discussion of what occurs in present-day publishing houses and its relationship to authorial diversity, see Zboray, "Books."

45. Two classic autobiographies are Goodrich, *Recollections of a Lifetime*; and James Cephas Derby, *Fifty Years among Authors, Books and Publishers* (New York: Carleton, 1884).

46. In preparing his *History of Book Publishing in the United States,* 4 vols. (New York: R. R. Bowker, 1972–81), John Tebbel mostly relied upon printed matter in the Frederic G. Melcher Library, company vertical files at R. R. Bowker, and a full run of *Publishers Weekly* (1:xi–xii).

47. Zboray, "Literary Enterprise and the Mass Market: Publishing and Business Innovation in Antebellum America," *Essays in Economic and Business History* 10 (1992): 168–81. The coordinated puffery is treated in William Charvat, "James T. Fields and the Beginnings of Book Promotion," *Huntington Library Quarterly* 8 (1944): 82–94.

48. For an analysis of Harper & Brothers's 1856 advertising records (published on microfilm by Chadwyck-Healey), see Zboray, *A Fictive People,* 63, table 5. For advertising records from an agency from the 1830s, see Homer & Palmer and Adams & Hudson account books in the Baker Business Library, Harvard University. One hundred fifteen posters from 1893 to 1907 are archived in the Posters for American Books and Magazines Collection, 1893–1907, Houghton Library, Harvard University.

49. See Charvat's account of the ramifications of Longfellow owning his own plates in *Profession of Authorship,* 159.

50. Papers at the American Antiquarian Society of Mathew Carey, McCarty & Davis, and West, Richardson & Lord were examined for chapter 4 of Zboray, *A Fictive People.* Bills, receipts, and invoices are also small bits of evidence to consider.

51. The Printer's File at the American Antiquarian Society provides details on printers' lives, their association with firms, and their imprints (most comprehensive for the years before 1820).

52. Deborah Cook, *The Culture Industry Revisited: Theodor W. Adorno on Mass Culture* (Lanham, Md.: Rowman & Littlefield, 1996).

53. For help in deciphering account books, see Robert J. Wilson III, *Early American Account Books: Interpretation, Cataloguing, and Use,* Technical Leaflet 140 (Nashville, Tenn.: American Association for State and Local History, n.d.).

54. A rich source for these manuscript account books is the five-volume collection "Account Books of Printers, Publishers, and Engravers, New England, 1798–1885," Baker Business Library, Harvard University.

55. David Clapp Jr., Journal, 1820–24, entry for 15 December 1822, Manuscript Department, Miscellaneous Manuscripts, box C, courtesy American Antiquarian Society.

56. Elizabeth Atherton Clapp, Journal, entries for 1 and 10 May 1852, Massachusetts Historical Society, Boston.

57. Examples of the manuscript materials can be found in the Manuscript Department of the American Antiquarian Society: Theodore Low De Vinne, Papers, 1883–1911, octavo vols., D [history and improvement of type]; Samuel N. Dickinson, Letters, 1841–49, Miscellaneous Manuscripts, box D; Phelps, Dalton & Co., Business Records, 1847–90, 2 vols., folio vols., P.

58. Dard Hunter, more than anyone else, pioneered modern analytical paper historiography and did so from the unique perspective of a craftsman able to produce fine paper.

59. Fredson Bowers, *Principles of Bibliographical Description* (Princeton, N.J.: Princeton University Press, 1949), 8. This book lays out the formulas for creating descriptive bibliographic notation and also describes the principles and distinguishing features of the discipline.

60. Fredson Bowers, *Bibliography and Textual Criticism* (Oxford: Clarendon Press, 1964), 4.

61. Roger E. Stoddard, *Marks in Books, Illustrated and Explained* (Cambridge, Mass.: Houghton Library, Harvard University, 1985), 2. This exhibition catalog is full of fascinating illustrations of the traces of usage upon books, including "inky fingerprints of the printers," 4–5.

62. D. F. McKenzie, *Bibliography and the Sociology of Texts* (Cambridge: Cambridge University Press, 1986), 8–13. Most studies of this type are based upon European books and therefore are in languages other than English (17n.8).

63. Frank E. Comparato, *Books for the Millions: A History of the Men Whose Methods and Machines Packaged the Printed Word* (Harrisburg, Pa.: Stackpole, 1971), 6–7. Cathy N. Davidson, for example, shows how *Charlotte Temple,* a popular early American novel, "could be repackaged in myriad ways"; see her "Life and Times of *Charlotte Temple*: The Biography of a Book," in *Reading in America: Literature and Social History* (Baltimore: Johns Hopkins University Press, 1989), 171–79.

64. Card files and record books are in the Copyright Office and the Rare Book and Special Collections Division of the Library of Congress.

65. For an extensive analysis of one bookstore's shelf inventory in antebellum New York, see chapter 10 in Zboray, *A Fictive People.*

66. W. Little & Co., *Programe of the Funeral Ceremonies in Honor of the Late President of the United States, 15 August 1850* (Boston: W. Little, 1850), broadside, courtesy American Antiquarian Society. We thank Richard D.

Brown for drawing our attention to this important piece. On periodical depots see Zboray, *A Fictive People,* 29–34.

67. For the journal of a book agent from Norwich, Conn., in Illinois, see William A. Gallup, Diaries, 1847–48, Connecticut Historical Society, Hartford.

68. J. A. Leo LeMay and P. M. Zall, eds., *The Autobiography of Benjamin Franklin: A Genetic Text* (Knoxville: University of Tennessee Press, 1981), 71–72.

69. Worcester Reading Club, 1849–1928, vol. 5 of Worcester (Mass.) Book Clubs Collection, 1844–1977, Manuscript Department, octavo vols., W, courtesy American Antiquarian Society.

70. For example, Norman A. Fletcher, account book of a general store in Bridport, Vt., 1839–40, and Bridport, Vt., Account Books of General Store, 1839–41, can be linked with Bridport Post Office, bound manuscript book listing newspapers and pamphlets received from 1 January 1839 to 31 December 1842 (all in Vermont Historical Society).

71. See, for example, George E. Littlefield, Auction Sales, 14 September 1839–12 February 1842, manuscript ledger, Rare Books and Manuscripts Room, Boston Public Library.

72. An analysis of two priced auction catalogs appears in Zboray, *A Fictive People,* 24–29.

73. Wolfgang Iser, *The Implied Reader: Patterns of Communication in Prose Fiction from Bunyan to Beckett* (Baltimore: Johns Hopkins University Press, 1974).

74. Steven Mailloux, "Misreading as a Historical Act: Cultural Rhetoric, Bible Politics, and Fuller's 1845 Review of Douglass's *Narrative,*" in *Readers in History: Nineteenth-Century American Literature and the Contexts of Response,* ed. James L. Machor (Baltimore: Johns Hopkins University Press, 1993), 13.

75. Stanley Fish, *Is There a Text in This Class?: The Authority of Interpretive Communities* (Cambridge, Mass.: Harvard University Press, 1980).

76. Janice A. Radway, *Reading the Romance: Women, Patriarchy, and Popular Literature* (Chapel Hill: University of North Carolina Press, 1984), is one such study in which the interview is conducted.

77. Karen V. Hansen and Cameron L. Macdonald, "Research Note: Surveying the Dead Informant: Analysis and Historical Interpretation," *Qualitative Sociology* 18 (1995): 227–36.

78. Cathy N. Davidson, *Revolution and the Word: The Rise of the Novel in America* (New York: Oxford University Press, 1986), 75, 77. Davidson looked at six thousand books for marginalia.

79. For example, see Archibald Stevens Alexander Library, Special Collections Department, *A Guide to Manuscript Diaries and Journals in the*

Special Collections Department, Rutgers University, comp. Donald D. Sinclair (New Brunswick, N.J.: Rutgers University Library, 1980).

80. William Matthews, *American Diaries: An Annotated Bibliography of American Diaries Written prior to the Year 1861* (Boston: J. S. Canner, 1959), ix. Such lists could contain over a thousand items; see, for example, John Pierce, "Book Lists," 1814–49, 1–68, Poor Family Papers, Schlesinger Library, Radcliffe College, Cambridge, Mass.

81. Susan K. Harris, *The Courtship of Olivia Langdon and Mark Twain* (Cambridge: Cambridge University Press, 1996), 93–134.

82. Ronald J. Zboray and Mary Saracino Zboray, "Books, Reading, and the World of Goods in Antebellum New England," *American Quarterly* 48 (December 1996): 587–622.

83. Charles T. Davis and Henry Louis Gates Jr., eds., *The Slave's Narrative* (Oxford: Oxford University Press, 1985), xii.

84. On the prevalence of the reading experience and the "talking book," see ibid., xxvii–xxix.

85. James Davie Butler, *Commonplace Books; Why and How Kept: A Lecture; With Suggestions on Object and Method in Reading* (Hartford, Conn.: Barnard's American Journal of Education, 1887), 11.

86. Kenneth A. Lockridge, *The Diary, and Life, of William Byrd II of Virginia, 1674–1744* (Chapel Hill: University of North Carolina Press, 1987), 48. For an analysis of some late nineteenth-century trade-card scrapbooks, see Ellen Gruber Garvey, *The Adman in the Parlor: Magazines and the Gendering of Consumer Culture, 1880s–1910s* (New York: Oxford University Press, 1998), chap. 1.

87. For one of the most dramatic examples of how a hunt for evidence of reading can produce a rich scholarship, see the sources on Transcendentalism in the Suggested Readings.

88. Lee Soltow and Edward Stevens, *The Rise of Literacy and the Common School in the United States: A Socioeconomic Analysis to 1870* (Chicago: University of Chicago Press, 1981), 1–2.

89. Carl F. Kaestle and others, *Literacy in the United States: Readers and Reading since 1880* (New Haven, Conn.: Yale University Press, 1991), 33.

90. E. Jennifer Monaghan, "Literacy Instruction and Gender in Colonial New England," in Davidson, *Reading in America,* 74.

91. Edward Stevens, "Illiterate Americans and Nineteenth-Century Courts: The Meanings of Literacy," in *Literacy in Historical Perspective,* ed. Daniel P. Resnick (Washington, D.C.: Library of Congress, 1983), 59–83. Boorstin quoted in Clement, *The Book in America,* 139.

92. Carol Buchalter Stapp, "Afro-Americans in Antebellum Boston: An Analysis of Probate Records," 2 vols. (Ph.D. diss., George Washington University, 1990), 1:36. Stapp transcribes some African American inven-

tories that contain lists of books (rosters 4 and 5, 2:651–54). She also considers other, related objects that suggest reading (like bookcases or maps) to correlate their presence in probates with occupation and signature marks (1:192–94).

93. William J. Gilmore, *Reading Becomes a Necessity of Life: Material and Cultural Life in Rural New England, 1780–1835* (Knoxville: University of Tennessee Press, 1989).

94. Ibid., 142–53.

95. P. J. Wallis, *Publications in Historical Biobibliography* (Newcastle upon Tyne, England: University of Newcastle upon Tyne, Department of Education, January 1980), 2.

96. Henry Bill Publishing Co., *The Henry Bill Publishing Co.'s Private Instructions to Their Agents for Selling Their Subscription Books* (Norwich, Conn.: Henry Bill Publishing Co., 1874[?]), 29; Janice A. Radway, *A Feeling for Books: The Book-of-the-Month Club, Literary Taste, and Middle-Class Desire* (Chapel Hill: University of North Carolina Press, 1997).

97. Thomas C. Leonard, *News for All: America's Coming-of-Age with the Press* (New York: Oxford University Press, 1995), 106–116.

98. A collaborative history is progressing under the auspices of the Library of Congress's Center for the Book under the editorship of Kenneth Carpenter of Harvard University and Wayne A. Wiegand of the University of Wisconsin.

99. *Bulletin of the Public Library of the City of Boston* (October 1867–January 1896), for example, gives accession lists.

100. David Paul Nord, "Systematic Benevolence: Religious Publishing and the Marketplace in Early Nineteenth-Century America," in *Communication and Change in American Religious History,* ed. Leonard I. Sweet (Grand Rapids, Mich.: William B. Eerdmans, 1993), 239–69.

101. Harold Bloom, *The Anxiety of Influence: A Theory of Poetry* (New York: Oxford University Press, 1973).

Suggested Readings

THE LITERATURE on book history in the United States is so vast that this list has to be highly selective. Since the list provides scholarly support for our discussion, we have organized it according to the main divisions of our text, but it does not contain every reference cited in the notes. Further, the list includes primary as well as secondary sources, since primary sources serve as examples. Most of the secondary sources treat American topics, but occasionally books and articles dealing with Europe are cited where American sources are lacking. Since the colonial period is best considered within the framework of British provincialism, sources from the period after independence dominate the list. Because our emphasis is historical, we have limited the number of references on the state of the book trades in the past decade or so. Our goal is to provide beginners with an array of sources that more or less represent the current state of book history in terms of approaches, not content. Hence, we did not seek full chronological or regional coverage for each division of the text. Scattered throughout the list are references that may not deal with book history per se, yet are methodologically essential.

I. INTRODUCTION

Brown, Richard D. *Knowledge Is Power: The Diffusion of Information in Early America, 1700–1865.* New York: Oxford University Press, 1989.

Charvat, William. *Literary Publishing in America, 1790–1850.* 1959; Amherst: University of Massachusetts Press, 1993.

Clement, Richard W. *The Book in America: With Images from the Library of Congress.* Golden, Colo.: Fulcrum Publishing, 1996.

Darnton, Robert. *The Business of Enlightenment: A Publishing History of the* Encyclopédie, *1775–1800*. Cambridge, Mass.: Belknap Press, 1979.

Davidson, Cathy N. *Revolution and Word: The Rise of the Novel in America.* New York: Oxford University Press, 1986.

Eisenstein, Elizabeth L. *The Printing Press as an Agent of Change: Communications and Cultural Transformations in Early Modern Europe.* 2 vols. Cambridge: Cambridge University Press, 1979.

Feather, John. *A Dictionary of Book History.* New York: Oxford University Press, 1986.

Feather, John P., and David McKitterick. *The History of Books and Libraries: Two Views.* Washington, D.C.: Library of Congress, 1986.

Gilmore, William J. *Reading Becomes a Necessity of Life: Material and Cultural Life in Rural New England, 1780–1835.* Knoxville: University of Tennessee Press, 1989.

Hall, David D. *Cultures of Print: Essays in the History of the Book.* Amherst: University of Massachusetts Press, 1996.

Hart, James D. *The Popular Book: A History of America's Literary Taste.* New York: Oxford University Press, 1950.

Innis, Harold. *Empire and Communications.* Oxford: Clarendon Press, 1950.

Joyce, William L., and others, eds. *Printing and Society in Early America.* Worcester, Mass.: American Antiquarian Society, 1983.

Lehmann-Haupt, Hellmut, Lawrence C. Wroth, and Rollo G. Silver. *The Book in America: A History of the Making and Selling of Books in the United States.* Second revised edition. New York: R. R. Bowker, 1951.

Martin, Henri-Jean, and Roger Chartier. *Histoire de l'édition française.* 4 vols. Paris: Promodis, 1983–86.

McLuhan, Marshall. *The Gutenberg Galaxy: The Making of Typographic Man.* Toronto: University of Toronto Press, 1962.

McMurtrie, Douglas C. *A History of Printing in the United States: The Story of the Introduction of the Press and of Its History and Influence during the Pioneer Period in Each State of the Union,* vol. 2, *Middle and South Atlantic States.* New York: R. R. Bowker, 1936.

Mott, Frank Luther. *Golden Multitudes: The Story of Best Sellers in the United States.* New York: Macmillan, 1947.

Olmert, Michael. *The Smithsonian Book of Books.* Washington, D.C.: Smithsonian Books, 1992.

Tebbel, John. *A History of Book Publishing in the United States.* 4 vols. New York: R. R. Bowker, 1972–81.

Thomas, Isaiah. *The History of Printing in America.* . . . 2 vols. Worcester, Mass.: Thomas, 1810.

Williams, Maurvene D., comp. *The Community of the Book: A Directory of Organizations and Programs.* Third edition. Washington, D.C.: Library of Congress, 1993.

Zboray, Ronald J. *A Fictive People: Antebellum Economic Development and the American Reading Public.* New York: Oxford University Press, 1993.

Zboray, Ronald J., and Mary Saracino Zboray. "Books, Reading, and the World of Goods in Antebellum New England." *American Quarterly* 48 (1996): 587–622.

———. "Transcendentalism in Print: Production, Dissemination, and Common Reception." In *Transient and Permanent: The Transcendentalist Movement and Its Contexts.* Edited by Charles Capper and Conrad Edick Wright. Boston: Massachusetts Historical Society, 1999.

II. HOW TO LOCATE AND USE SOURCES

A. WHERE TO BEGIN

1. *General Sources*

Cole, John Y., ed. *In Celebration: The National Union Catalog, Pre-1956 Imprints.* Washington, D.C.: Library of Congress, 1981.

Library of Congress. *National Union Catalog: Pre-1956 Imprints.* . . . 754 vols. London: Mansell, 1968–81.

Schreyer, Alice D. *The History of Books: A Guide to Selected Resources in the Library of Congress.* Washington, D.C.: Center for the Book, Library of Congress, 1987.

Smith, David A. "The National Union Catalog: Pre-1956 Imprints." *Book Collector* 31 (1982): 445–62.

a. Bibliographies

Annual Bibliography of the History of the Printed Book and Libraries. The Hague: Martinus Nijhoff, 1970–.

Tanselle, G. Thomas. *Guide to the Study of United States Imprints.* 2 vols. Cambridge, Mass.: Belknap Press of Harvard University Press, 1971.

b. Imprint Lists

Books in Print. New York: R. R. Bowker, 1948–.

Evans, Charles. *American Bibliography: A Chronological Dictionary of All*

Books, Pamphlets, and Periodical Publications Printed in the United States of America from the Genesis of Printing in 1639 down to and Including the Year 1820 [1800]. 15 vols. Chicago: private printing, 1903–34; Worcester, Mass.: American Antiquarian Society, 1955, 1959, 1961.

Kelly, James. *The American Catalogue of Books (Original and Reprints) Published in the United States from Jan., 1861, to Jan., [1871].* 2 vols. New York: J. Wiley & Son, 1866–71.

The Publishers' Trade List Annual. New York: Publishers Weekly, later R. R. Bowker, 1874–.

Rinderknecht, Carol. *A Checklist of American Imprints for 1830–39: Author Title Indexes.* 4 vols. Metuchen, N.J.: Scarecrow, 1989.

Roorbach, Orville. *Bibliotheca Americana: Catalogue of American Publications, including Reprints and Original Works, from 1820 to 1852, Inclusive.* [Various supplements and editions to 1861.] New York: Roorbach, 1849–61.

R. R. Bowker Co., Department of Bibliography. *American Book Publishing Record, 1876–1949: An American National Bibliography.* 15 vols. New York: R. R. Bowker, 1980.

Sabin, Joseph. *Dictionary of Books Relating to America, from Its Discovery to the Present Time.* 29 vols. New York: Joseph Sabin; Philadelphia: John Campbell; London: N. Trübner, 1868–1937.

Shaw, Ralph, and Richard H. Shoemaker. *American Bibliography: A Preliminary Checklist for 1801* [through 1819]. 19 vols. New York: Scarecrow Press, 1958–63.

Shoemaker, Richard H. *A Checklist of American Imprints for 1820–1829.* New York: Scarecrow Press, 1964–71.

c. Trade Papers

Norton, Charles B., ed. *Norton's Literary Gazette and Publishers' Circular.* New York: Norton, 1851–55.

Publishers Weekly. New York: R. R. Bowker, 1873–.

Zboray, Ronald J. "Book Distribution and American Culture: A 150-Year Perspective." *Book Research Quarterly* 3 (1987): 37–59.

d. Trade Directories

NOTE: See Tanselle, *Guide to the Study of United States Imprints,* for specific citations to 1970.

American Booktrade Directory. New York: R. R. Bowker, 1925–.

Bristol, Roger P. *Index of Printers, Publishers, and Booksellers Indicated by Charles Evans in His American Bibliography*. Charlottesville: Bibliographical Society of the University of Virginia, 1961.

Franklin, Benjamin, V, comp. *Boston Printers, Publishers, and Booksellers: 1640–1800*. Boston: G. K. Hall, 1980.

Huttner, Sidney F., and Elizabeth S. Huttner. *A Register of Artists, Engravers, Booksellers, Bookbinders, Printers and Publishers in New York City, 1821–42*. New York: Bibliographical Society of America, 1993.

Phelps, C. Deirdre. "Printing, Publishing, and Bookselling in Salem, Massachusetts, 1825–1900." *Essex Institute Historical Collections* 124 (1988): 227–95.

Printing Trades Blue Book. New York: A. F. Lewis, 1916–.

Zboray, Ronald J., and Mary Saracino Zboray. The Boston Book Trades Database, 1789–1850. [Computer file, in process to 1861.] Department of History, Georgia State University.

————. "The Boston Book Trade, 1789–1850: A Statistical and Geographical Analysis." In *Entrepreneurs: The Boston Business Community, 1700–1850*. Edited by Conrad Edick Wright and Katheryn P. Viens. Boston: Massachusetts Historical Society, 1997.

e. City Directories and Census Materials

City and Business Directories of the United States through 1860. [Microform.] New Haven, Conn.: Research Publications, 1966–.

Spear, Dorothea N. *Bibliography of American Directories through 1860*. Worcester, Mass.: American Antiquarian Society, 1961.

f. Newspapers and Other Serials

American Periodicals, 1741–1900. Ann Arbor, Mich.: University Microfilms International, 1979–.

Anderson, Elizabeth L., ed. *Newspaper Libraries in the U.S. and Canada*. Second edition. New York: Special Libraries Association, 1980.

Brigham, Clarence S. *History and Bibliography of American Newspapers, 1690–1820*. Revised edition. 2 vols. Worcester, Mass.: American Antiquarian Society, 1947.

Cushing, Helen Grant, and Adah V. Morris, eds. *Nineteenth Century Readers' Guide to Periodical Literature, 1890–1899: With Supplemental Indexing, 1900–1922*. New York: H. W. Wilson, 1944.

Gregory, Winifred. *American Newspapers, 1821–1936: A Union List of Files*

Available in the United States and Canada. New York: H. W. Wilson, 1937.

――――. *Union List of Serials in the Libraries of the United States and Canada.* Third edition. Edited by Edna Brown Titus. 5 vols. New York: H. W. Wilson, 1965.

Hoornstra, Jean, and Trudy Heath. *American Periodicals, 1741–1900: An Index to the Microfilm Collections—American Periodicals Nineteenth Century, American Periodicals, 1800–1850, American Periodicals, 1850–1900, Civil War and Reconstruction.* Ann Arbor: University Microfilms International, 1979.

Kellerman, Lydia Suzanne, and Rebecca A. Wilson. *Index to Readex Microfilm Collection of Early American Newspapers.* New Canaan, Conn.: Readex, 1990.

Kribbs, Jayne K., comp. *An Annotated Bibliography of American Literary Periodicals, 1741–1850.* Boston: G. K. Hall, 1977.

Milner, Anita Cheek, ed. *Newspaper Indexes: A Location and Subject Guide for Researchers.* 3 vols. Metuchen, N.J.: Scarecrow Press, 1977–82.

Newspapers in Microform, United States, 1948–1983. 2 vols. Washington, D.C.: Library of Congress, 1984.

Readers' Guide to Periodical Literature. Minneapolis, Minn., White Plains, N.Y., and New York: H. W. Wilson, 1900–.

Schwarzlose, Richard. *The Nation's Newsbrokers.* 2 vols. Evanston, Ill.: Northwestern University Press, 1989–90.

――――. *Newspapers, A Reference Guide.* New York: Greenwood Press, 1987.

The Serials Directory: An International Reference Book. Second edition. 3 vols. Birmingham, Ala.: EBSCO, 1987.

Ulrich's International Periodicals Directory. New York: R. R. Bowker, 1965–.

Wall, C. Edward, ed. and comp. *Cumulative Author Index for Poole's Index to Periodical Literature, 1802–1906.* Ann Arbor, Mich.: Pierian Press, 1971.

g. Other Business / Public Sources

Bankrupt Register: A Record of Law Reports and Proceedings in All of the States [later *National Bankruptcy Register*]. New York: G. T. Deller, 1868–82.

The Gazette and Bankrupt Court Reporter. New York: Donogh & Black, 1867–.

Norris, James D. *R. G. Dun & Co., 1841–1900: The Development of Credit*

Reporting in the Nineteenth Century. Westport, Conn.: Greenwood Press, 1978.

R. G. Dun & Co. Credit Ledgers, 1840–95. Baker Business Library, Harvard University.

2. *Genre-Specific Sources*

a. *Trade Fiction and Poetry*

NOTE: See also Hart and Mott citations above, section I. Introduction.

American Fiction, 1774–1875. [Microfilm.] Ann Arbor, Mich.: University Microfilms, 1966–.

American Poetry, 1609–1900: A Collection on Microfilm. Woodbridge, Conn.: Research Publications, 1976–.

Blanck, Jacob. *Bibliography of American Literature.* 9 vols. New Haven, Conn.: Yale University Press, 1955–91. [Contains belles-lettres, as well.]

Cohen, Daniel A. *Pillars of Salt, Monuments of Grace: New England Crime Literature and the Origins of American Popular Culture, 1674–1860.* New York: Oxford University Press, 1993.

Dime-Novel Round-up. Lawrence, Kans.: Happy Hours Brotherhood, 1931–.

Faxon, Frederick W. *Literary Annuals and Gift Books: A Bibliography, 1823–1903.* 1912; Pinner, Eng.: Private Libraries Association, 1973.

Hackett, Alice Payne. *Fifty Years of Best Sellers, 1895–1945.* New York: R. R. Bowker, 1945.

Hubin, Allen J. *Crime Fiction, 1749–1980: A Comprehensive Bibliography.* New York and London: Garland, 1984.

Irish, Wynot R. *The Modern American Muse: A Complete Bibliography of American Verse, 1900–1925.* Syracuse: Syracuse University Press, 1950.

Johannsen, Albert. *The House of Beadle & Adams and Its Dime and Nickel Novels: The Story of a Vanished Literature.* 3 vols. Norman: University of Oklahoma Press, 1950–62.

Kirkham, E. Bruce, and John W. Fink, comps. *Indices to American Literary Annuals and Gift Books, 1825–1865.* New Haven, Conn.: Research Publications, 1975.

McPehron, William. *The Bibliography of Contemporary American Poetry, 1945–1985: An Annotated Checklist.* Westport, Conn.: Meckler, 1986.

Miller, William Cleveland. *Dime Novel Authors, 1860–1900.* Grafton, Mass.: R. F. Cummings, 1933.

Rogers, Denis R. *The American Novels.* Fall River, Mass.: E. T. LeBlanc, 1981.

Schick, Frank L. *The Paperbound Book in America: The History of Paperbacks and Their European Background.* New York: R. R. Bowker, 1958.

Thompson, Ralph. *American Literary Annuals and Gift Books, 1825–1865.* New York: H. W. Wilson, 1936.

Wegelin, Oscar. *Early American Poetry: A Compilation of the Titles and Volumes of Verse and Broadsides by Writers Born or Residing in North America, North of the Mexican Border.* Second edition. 2 vols. New York: Peter Smith, 1930.

Wright, Lyle, *American Fiction, 1774–1850, 1851–1875, and 1876–1900: A Contribution toward a Bibliography.* 3 vols. San Marino, Calif.: Huntington Library, 1969, 1965, 1966.

b. Trade Nonfiction

Beers, Henry Putney. *Bibliographies in American History: Guide to Materials for Research.* Second edition. New York: H. W. Wilson, 1942.

———. *Bibliographies in American History, 1942–1978: Guide to Materials for Research.* 2 vols. Woodbridge, Conn.: Research Publications, 1982.

Bliss, Carey S. *Autos across America: A Bibliography of Transcontinental Automobile Travel, 1903–40.* Austin, Tex.: Jenks & Reese, 1982.

Casper, Scott E. *Constructing American Lives: Biography and Culture in Nineteenth-Century America.* Chapel Hill: University of North Carolina Press, 1999.

Cole, John Y., ed. *Biography and Books: Papers Originally Presented at a Symposium Held Nov. 9–10, 1983, at the Library of Congress and Sponsored by the Center for the Book.* Washington, D.C.: Library of Congress, 1986.

Cox, Edward Godfrey. *A Reference Guide to the Literature of Travel: Including Voyages, Geographical Descriptions, Adventures, Shipwrecks and Expeditions,* 3 vols. Seattle: University of Washington, 1935–49.

Danzer, Gerald A. "America's Roots in the Past: Historical Publication in America to 1860." Ph.D. diss., Northwestern University, 1967.

Dargan, Marion. *Guide to American Biography.* 2 vols. Albuquerque: University of New Mexico Press, 1949–52.

Dougherty, James L. *Writings on American History, 1962–73: A Subject Bibliography of Articles.* 4 vols. Washington, D.C.: American Historical Association, 1976.

Downs, Robert Bingham. *Images of America: Travelers from Abroad in the New World*. Urbana: University of Illinois Press, 1987.

Henline, Ruth. "Travel Literature of Colonists in America, 1754–1783: An Annotated Bibliography and an Author Index." Ph.D. diss., Northwestern University, 1947.

Kagle, Steven E. *America: Exploration and Travel*. Bowling Green, Ohio: Bowling Green State University Popular Press, 1979.

Kaplan, Louis. *A Bibliography of American Autobiographies*. Madison: University of Wisconsin Press, 1962.

Monaghan, Frank. *French Travellers in the United States, 1765–1932*. New York: New York Public Library, 1933.

O'Neill, Edward H. *Biography by Americans, 1658–1936: A Subject Bibliography*. Philadelphia: University of Pennsylvania Press, 1939.

Smith, Harold Frederick. *American Travellers Abroad: A Bibliography of Accounts Published before 1900*. Carbondale: Southern Illinois University Library, 1969.

Tobias, Barbara, Mary Louise Briscoe, and Lynn Z. Bloom. *American Autobiography, 1945–1980: A Bibliography*. Madison: University of Wisconsin Press, 1982.

Wagner, Henry R. *The Plains and the Rockies: A Bibliography of Original Narratives of Travel and Adventure, 1800–1865*. 1920; San Francisco: Grabhorn Press, 1937.

Wile, Annadel N. *C.R.I.S.: The Combined Retrospective Index Set to Journals in History, 1838–1974*. 11 vols. [vols. 5–9 dealing with U.S. history]. Washington, D.C.: Carrollton Press, 1977–78.

c. Children's Books

Association for Library Service to Children. *Special Collections in Children's Literature, An International Directory*. Third edition. Chicago: American Library Association, 1995.

Baldwin, Ruth M. *Index to the Baldwin Library of Books in English before 1900 Primarily for Children, University of Florida Libraries, Gainesville*. 3 vols. Boston: G. K. Hall, 1981.

Haviland, Virginia. *Children's Literature: A Guide to Reference Sources* [with 2 supplements]. Washington, D.C.: Library of Congress, 1966, 1972, 1977.

Library of Congress. *Children's Books in the Rare Book Division of the Library of Congress*. 2 vols. Totowa, N.J.: Rowman & Littlefield, 1975.

Welch, D'Alté A. *A Bibliography of American Children's Books Printed Prior to 1821.* 1963; Worcester, Mass.: American Antiquarian Society, 1972.

d. Textbooks

American Primers. [Microfiche.] Frederick, Md.: University Publications of America, 1990.

Booth, David W. *Censorship Goes to School.* Markham, Ont.: Pembroke, 1992.

Carpenter, Charles. *The History of American Schoolbooks.* Philadelphia: University of Pennsylvania Press, 1963.

Cole, John Y., and Thomas G. Sticht, eds. *The Textbook in American Society: A Volume Based on a Conference at the Library of Congress on May 2–3, 1979.* Washington, D.C.: Library of Congress, 1979.

DelFattore, Joan. *What Johnny Shouldn't Read: Textbook Censorship in America.* New Haven, Conn.: Yale University Press, 1992.

Elson, Ruth Miller. *Guardians of Tradition: American Schoolbooks of the Nineteenth Century.* Lincoln: University of Nebraska Press, 1964.

FitzGerald, Frances. *America Revised: History Schoolbooks in the Twentieth Century.* Boston: Little, Brown, 1979.

Foerstel, Herbert N. *Banned in the U.S.A.: A Reference Guide to Book Censorship in School and Public Libraries.* Westport, Conn.: Greenwood Press, 1994.

Jenkinson, Edward B. *Censors in the Classroom: The Mind Benders.* Carbondale: Southern Illinois University Press, 1979.

Lawler, Thomas Bonaventure. *Seventy Years of Textbook Publishing: A History of Ginn & Company, 1867–1937.* Boston: Ginn & Co., 1938.

Littell, Joseph F. *A Lifetime in Every Moment.* Boston: Houghton Mifflin, 1995.

Monaghan, Charles. *The Murrays of Murray Hill.* Brooklyn, N.Y.: Urban History Press, 1998.

Monaghan, E. Jennifer. *A Common Heritage: Noah Webster's Blue-Back Speller.* Hamden, Conn.: Archon Books, 1983.

Nietz, John Alfred. *The Evolution of American Secondary School Textbooks . . . before 1900.* Rutland, Vt.: C. E. Tuttle, 1966.

Svobodny, Dolly. *Early American Textbooks, 1775–1900: A Catalogue of Titles Held by the Educational Research Library.* Washington, D.C.: U.S. Department of Education, 1985.

Westerhoff, John H., III. *McGuffey and His Readers: Piety, Morality, and*

Education in Nineteenth-Century America. Nashville, Tenn.: Abingdon, 1978.

Woodward, Arthur. *Textbooks in School and Society: An Annotated Bibliography and Guide to Research.* New York: Garland, 1988.

e. Academic Books

American Association of University Presses. *Directory.* New York: AAUP, 1952–.

Hall, Max. *Harvard University Press: A History.* Cambridge, Mass.: Harvard University Press, 1986.

Jeanneret, Marsh. *God and Mammon: Universities as Publishers.* Toronto: Macmillan, 1989.

Machlup, Fritz. *Information through the Printed Word: The Dissemination of Scholarly, Scientific, and Intellectual Knowledge.* 4 vols. New York: Praeger, 1978–80.

Oleson, Alexandra, and Sanborn C. Brown, eds. *The Pursuit of Knowledge in the Early American Republic: American Scientific and Learned Societies from Colonial Times to the Civil War.* Baltimore: Johns Hopkins University Press, 1976.

Oleson, Alexandra, and John Voss, eds. *The Organization of Knowledge in Modern America, 1860–1920.* Baltimore: Johns Hopkins University Press, 1979.

One Book/Five Ways: The Publishing Procedures of Five University Presses. Los Altos, Calif.: Kaufmann, 1978.

Parsons, Paul. *Getting Published: The Acquisition Process at University Presses.* Knoxville: University of Tennessee Press, 1989.

Scholarly Publishing. Toronto: University of Toronto Press, 1969–.

University Publishing. Berkeley, Calif.: University Press Books/Berkeley, 1976–84.

f. Scientific, Technical, Medical, and Legal Books

Austin, Robert B. *Early American Medical Imprints: A Guide to Works Printed in the United States, 1668–1820.* Washington, D.C.: U.S. Department of Health, Education, and Welfare, 1961.

Channell, David F. *The History of Engineering Science: An Annotated Bibliography.* New York: Garland, 1989.

Cohen, Morris L. *Bibliography of Early American Law.* 6 vols. Buffalo, N.Y.: William S. Hein, 1998.

Cordasco, Francesco. *American Medical Imprints, 1820–1910.* . . . 2 vols. Totowa, N.J.: Rowman & Littlefield, 1985.

————. *Medical Publishing in Nineteenth-Century America: Lea of Philadelphia, William Wood & Co. of New York City, and F. E. Boericke of Philadelphia.* . . . Fairview, N.J.: Junius-Vaughn, 1990.

Crane, Edward Matthews. *A Century of Book Publishing, 1848–1949.* New York: Van Nostrand, 1948.

Dusseau, John L. *An Informal History of W. B. Saunders Company on the Occasion of Its Hundredth Anniversary.* Philadelphia: W. B. Saunders, 1988.

Ferguson, Eugene S., ed. *Bibliography of the History of Technology.* Cambridge, Mass.: Society for the History of Technology and MIT Press, 1968.

Friend, William Lawrence. *Anglo-American Legal Bibliographies: An Annotated Guide.* 1944; South Hackensack, N.J.: Rothman, 1966.

Goedan, Jurgen Christoph. *International Legal Bibliographies: A Worldwide Guide and Critique.* Ardsley-on-Hudson, N.Y.: Transnational Publishers, 1992.

Gross, Michael. *A Pocket Tour of Law on the Internet.* San Francisco: Sybex, 1995.

Guerra, Francisco. *American Medical Bibliography, 1639–1783.* . . . New York: Lathrop C. Harper, 1962.

Hawkins, R. R. *Scientific, Medical, and Technical Books Published in the United States of America* . . . *, 1930–1944, 1945–1948, 1949–1950.* Washington, D.C.: National Research Council, 1946, 1950, 1953; second edition, 1958.

Karpinksi, Louis C. *Bibliography of Mathematical Works Printed in America through 1850.* Ann Arbor: University of Michigan Press, 1940.

Law Books, 1876–1981: Books and Serials on Law and Its Related Subjects. New York: R. R. Bowker, 1981.

Miller, Genevieve, ed. *Bibliography of the History of Medicine of the United States and Canada, 1939–1960.* Baltimore: Johns Hopkins University Press, 1964.

Nineteenth-Century Legal Treatises. Woodbridge, Conn.: Research Publications, 1984–.

Ritz, Wilfred J. *American Judicial Proceedings First Printed before 1801: An Analytical Bibliography.* Westport, Conn.: Greenwood Press, 1984.

Rogers, Harriet C. "Books in Medicine, Botany, and Chemistry Printed in the American Colonies and the United States before 1801: A

Study of the Rise of Scientific Publishing in America during the Seventeenth and Eighteenth Centuries, with an Appended Check-List of Imprints (1668–1800)." M.L.S. thesis, Columbia University, 1932.

Rothenberg, Marc. *The History of Science and Technology in the United States: A Critical and Selective Bibliography.* 2 vols. New York: Garland, 1982–93.

Schmeck, Harold M. *Karger, Turning Medical Progress into Print: A Mirror of a Century of Medical and Scientific Publishing.* Basel, Switzerland: Karger, 1990.

Twentieth-Century Legal Treatises. Woodbridge, Conn.: Research Publications, 1995–.

U.S. National Library of Medicine [John Shaw Billings]. *Index-Catalogue of the Library of the Surgeon-General's Office, United States Army; Authors and Subjects.* 1st–5th series. Washington, D.C.: Government Printing Office, 1880–1961.

Whitrow, Magda, ed. Isis *Cumulative Bibliography: A Bibliography of the History of Science formed from* Isis *Critical Bibliographies 1–90, 1913–65.* 6 vols. London: Mansell and History of Science Society, 1971–84.

g. Reference Books

Arner, Robert D. *Dobson's Encyclopedia: The Publisher, Text, and Publication of America's First* Britannica, *1789–1803.* Philadelphia: University of Pennsylvania Press, 1991.

Balay, Robert, ed. *Guide to Reference Books.* Eleventh edition. Chicago: American Library Association, 1996.

Brown, Eleanor, and Bob Brown. *Culinary Americana: Cookbooks Published in the Cities and Towns of the United States of America during the Years from 1860 through 1960.* New York: Roving Eye Press, 1961.

Collison, Robert. *Encyclopedias: Their History through the Ages; A Bibliographic Guide. . . .* New York: Hafner, 1964.

Henderson, Robert W. *Early American Sport: A Checklist of Books by American and Foreign Authors Published in America Prior to 1860 including Sporting Songs.* Third revised edition. Rutherford, N.J.: Fairleigh Dickinson Press, 1977.

International Maps and Atlases in Print. London and New York: R. R. Bowker, 1974–.

Le Gear, Clare Egli. *United States Atlases: A List of National, State, County, City, and Regional Atlases in the Library of Congress.* Washington, D.C.: Library of Congress, 1950–.

Lowenstein, Eleanor. *Bibliography of American Cookery Books, 1742–1860.* Third edition. Worcester, Mass.: American Antiquarian Society, 1972.

Mukerji, Chandra. *From Graven Images: Patterns of Modern Materialism.* New York: Columbia University Press, 1983.

National Union Catalog. Cartographic Materials. [Microform.] Washington, D.C.: Library of Congress, 1983–.

O'Neill, Robert Keating. *English-Language Dictionaries, 1604–1900.* New York: Greenwood Press, 1988.

Phillips, John C. *American Game Mammals and Birds: A Catalogue of Books, 1582 to 1925, Sport, Natural History, Conservation.* Boston: Houghton Mifflin, 1930.

Phillips, P. Lee. *List of Maps of America in the Library of Congress.* Washington, D.C.: Government Printing Office, 1901.

Sader, Marion, and Amy Lewis, eds. *Encyclopedias, Atlases and Dictionaries.* New Providence, N.J.: R. R. Bowker, 1995.

Walsh, S. Padraig. *Anglo-American General Encyclopedias: A Historical Bibliography, 1703–1967.* New York: R. R. Bowker, 1968.

h. Religious Books

Albaugh, Gaylord. *History and Annotated Bibliography of American Religious Periodicals and Newspapers Established from 1730 through 1830.* 2 vols. Worcester, Mass.: American Antiquarian Society, 1994.

Barrow, John G. *A Bibliography of Bibliographies in Religion.* Ann Arbor, Mich.: Edwards Brothers, 1955.

Bruner, Helen M. *An Annotated Bibliography of Sermons and Tracts Delivered in New England between 1720 and 1810.* San Francisco: California State Library, 1939.

Hatch, Nathan O., and Mark A. Noll, eds. *The Bible in America: Essays in Cultural History.* New York: Oxford University Press, 1982.

Hills, Margaret T. *The English Bible in America: A Bibliography of Editions of the Bible and the New Testament Published in America, 1777–1957.* New York: American Bible Society, 1961.

Howsam, Leslie. *Cheap Bibles: Nineteenth-Century Publishing and the British and Foreign Bible Society.* Cambridge: Cambridge University Press, 1991.

Hurst, John F. *Bibliotheca Theologica: A Select and Classified Bibliography of Theology and General Religious Literature.* New York: C. Scribner's, 1883.

Kepple, Robert J. *Reference Works for Theological Research*. Third edition. Lanham, Md.: University Press of America, 1991.

Moore, R. Laurence. "Religion, Secularization, and the Shaping of the Culture Industry in Antebellum America." *American Quarterly* 41 (1989): 216–42.

Nord, David Paul. "The Evangelical Origins of Mass Media in America, 1815–1835." *Journalism Monographs* 88. Columbia, S.C.: Association for Education in Journalism, 1984.

Norton, Luke Wesley. *Religious Newspapers in the Old Northwest to 1861: A History, Bibliography, and Record of Opinion*. Athens: Ohio University Press, 1977.

Reynolds, David S. *Faith in Fiction: The Emergence of Religious Literature in America*. Cambridge, Mass.: Harvard University Press, 1981.

Smith, Wilbur Moorhead. "A Bibliography of Biblical, Ecclesiastical, and Theological Dictionaries and Encyclopedias Published in Great Britain and America." *Fuller Library Bulletin* 20–23 (October 1953–September 1954): 4–30.

Sweet, Leonard I., ed. *Communication and Change in American Religious History*. Grand Rapids, Mich.: Eerdmans, 1993.

Wosh, Peter J. *Spreading the Word: The Bible Business in Nineteenth-Century America*. Ithaca, N.Y.: Cornell University Press, 1994.

Wright, John. *Early Prayer Books of America. . . .* St. Paul, Minn.: private printing, 1896.

i. Business Books

Bentley, Harry C., and Ruth S. Leonard. *Bibliography of Works on Accounting by American Authors*. 2 vols. Boston: H. C. Bentley, 1924–35.

Daniells, Lorna M., comp. *Studies in Enterprise: A Selected Bibliography of American and Canadian Company Histories and Biographies of Business Men*. Boston: Baker Library, Harvard University, Graduate School of Business, 1957.

Davis, Alec. *Package and Print: The Development of Container and Label Design*. New York: C. N. Potter, 1968.

Dillistin, William H. *Bank Note Reporters and Counterfeit Detectors, 1826–1866*. New York: American Numismatic Society, 1949.

Edwards, Everett Eugene. *A Bibliography of the History of Agriculture in the United States*. Washington, D.C.: U.S. Department of Agriculture, 1930.

Endres, Kathleen L. *Trade, Industrial, and Professional Periodicals of the United States.* Westport, Conn.: Greenwood Press, 1994.

Fisher, William. *Business Journals of the United States.* New York: Greenwood Press, 1991.

Forsyth, David P. *The Business Press in America.* Philadelphia: Chilton Books, 1964.

Hine, Thomas. *The Total Package: The Evolution and Secret Meanings of Boxes, Bottles, Cans, and Tubes.* Boston: Little, Brown, 1995.

Hollander, Stanley C. *History of Labels: A Record of the Past Developed in the Search for the Origins of an Industry.* New York: A. Hollander, 1956.

Jay, Robert. *The Trade Card in Nineteenth-Century America.* Columbia: University of Missouri Press, 1987.

Larson, Henrietta M. *Guide to Business History: Materials for the Study of American Business History and Suggestions for Their Use.* Cambridge, Mass.: Harvard University Press, 1948.

Pollay, Richard W., ed. *Information Sources in Advertising History.* Westport, Conn.: Greenwood Press, 1979.

Romaine, Lawrence B. *A Guide to American Trade Catalogs, 1744–1900.* New York: R. R. Bowker, 1960.

R. R. Bowker Co., *Business and Economics Books, 1876–1983.* 4 vols. New York: Bowker, 1983.

Schlebecker, John T. *Bibliography of Books and Pamphlets on the History of Agriculture in the United States, 1607–1967.* Santa Barbara, Calif.: ABC-Clio, 1969.

Taber, Thomas T., III, comp. *Guide to Railroad Historical Resources: United States and Canada.* 4 vols. Muncy, Pa.: private printing, 1993.

Tucher, Andrea J., comp. *Agriculture in America, 1622–1860. . . .* New York: Garland, 1984.

j. Specialty Publishing

Ahlquist, Karen. *Democracy at the Opera: Music, Theater, and Culture in New York City, 1815–1860.* Urbana: University of Illinois Press, 1997.

Broyles, Michael. *Music of the Highest Class: Elitism and Populism in Antebellum Boston.* New Haven, Conn.: Yale University Press, 1992.

Buday, Gyorgy. *The History of the Christmas Card.* London: Rockliff, 1954.

Gillespie, John, and Anna Gillespie. *A Bibliography of Nineteenth-Century American Piano Music, with Location Sources and Composer Biography-Index.* Westport, Conn.: Greenwood Press, 1984.

Hall, James William. "The Tune-Book in American Culture, 1800–1820." Ph.D. diss., University of Pennsylvania, 1967.

Hargrave, Catherine Perry. *A History of Playing Cards and a Bibliography of Cards and Gaming.* Boston and New York: Houghton Mifflin, 1930.

Haskell, Francis. *The Painful Birth of the Art Book.* London: Thames & Hudson, 1987.

Horn, David. *The Literature of American Music in Books and Folk Music Collections: A Fully Annotated Bibliography.* Metuchen, N.J.: Scarecrow Press, 1977.

Hunter, David, ed. *Music Publishing and Collecting: Essays in Honor of Donald W. Krummel.* Urbana: Graduate School of Library and Information Science, University of Illinois at Urbana-Champaign, 1994.

Janse, William Morton. *The History of Valentines: An Historical Account of the Origin, Evolution, Development, and Value of Valentines from Earliest Days to the Present Time.* Chatham, Mass.: private printing, 1950.

Krummel, Donald W. *Bibliographical Handbook of American Music.* Urbana: University of Illinois Press, 1987.

———. *The Literature of Music Bibliography: An Account of the Writings on the History of Music, Printing and Publishing.* Berkeley, Calif.: Fallen Leaf Press, 1992.

———. *The Memory of Sound: Observations on the History of Music on Paper.* Washington, D.C.: Library of Congress, 1988.

Krummel, Donald W., and others. *Resources of American Music History: A Directory of Source Materials from Colonial Times to World War II.* Urbana: University of Illinois Press, 1981.

Lawrence, Vera Brodsky. *Strong on Music: The New York Music Scene in the Days of George Templeton Strong, 1836–1875.* 2 vols. New York: Oxford University Press, 1988–.

Loesser, Arthur. *Men, Women, and Pianos: A Social History.* New York: Simon & Schuster, 1954.

Sanjek, Russell. *American Popular Music and Its Business: The First Four Hundred Years.* 3 vols. New York: Oxford University Press, 1988.

———. *From Print to Plastic: Publishing and Promoting America's Popular Music (1900–1980).* Brooklyn, N.Y.: Institute for Studies in American Music, Conservatory of Music, Brooklyn College of the City University of New York, 1983.

Sonneck, Oscar. *A Bibliography of Early Secular Music (Eighteenth Century).* Revised and enlarged by William Treat Upton. 1909; Washington, D.C.: Library of Congress, Music Division, 1945.

————. *Oscar Sonneck and American Music.* Edited by William Lichten-wanger. Urbana: University of Illinois Press, 1983.

Staff, Frank. *The Valentine and Its Origins.* New York: Praeger, 1969.

Weiss, Morry. *American Greetings Corporation.* New York: Newcomen Society in North America, 1982.

k. Other Private Sector

Bowker, R. R. *Publications of Societies: A Provisional List of the Publications of American Scientific, Literary, and Other Societies from Their Organization.* New York: Publishers' Weekly, 1899.

Marshall, John. *Publication of Books and Monographs by Learned Societies.* Washington, D.C.: American Council of Learned Societies, 1931.

Neufield, Maurice F., Daniel J. Leab, and Dorothy Swanson. *American Working Class History: A Representative Bibliography.* New York: R. R. Bowker, 1983.

Reynolds, Lloyd G., and Charles C. Killingsworth. *Trade Union Publications: The Official Journals, Convention Proceedings, and Constitutions of International Unions and Federations, 1850–1941.* 3 vols. Baltimore: Johns Hopkins University Press, 1944.

Whitehill, Walter Muir. *Independent Historical Societies: An Inquiry into Their Research and Publication Functions and Their Financial Future.* Boston: The Boston Athenæum; distributed by Harvard University Press, 1962.

l. Government

Bowker, Richard R. *State Publications: A Provisional List of the Official Publications of the Several States of the United States from Their Organization.* 2 vols. New York: Office of the Publishers' Weekly, 1899–1908.

Boyd, Anne Morris. *United States Government Publications.* Third edition. New York: Wilson, 1949.

Childs, James B. *An Account of Government Document Bibliography in the United States and Elsewhere.* Third edition. Washington, D.C.: Government Printing Office, 1942.

Hodgson, James Goodwin. *The Official Publications of American Counties: A Union List.* [Mimeograph.] Fort Collins, Colo.: Hodgson, 1937.

Manvel, Allen D. *Checklist of Basic Municipal Documents.* Census Bureau State and Local Government Special Studies 27. Washington, D.C.: Government Printing Office, 1948.

Monthly [Check-]List of State Publications. Washington, D.C.: Government Printing Office, 1910–.

Morehead, Joe. *Introduction to United States Government Information Sources.* Fifth edition. Englewood, Colo.: Libraries Unlimited, 1996.

Palic, Vladimir M. *Government Publications: A Guide to Bibliographic Tools.* Fourth edition. Washington, D.C.: Library of Congress, 1975.

Powell, John Harvey. *The Books of a New Nation: United States Government Publications, 1774–1814.* Philadelphia: University of Pennsylvania Press, 1957.

Schmeckebier, Laurence F., and Roy B. Eastin. *Government Publications and Their Use.* Washington, D.C.: Brookings Institution, 1969.

m. Translations and Imitations

Clegg's International Directory of the World's Book Trade. London: J. Clarke and others, 1886–1950.

Cumulative Index to English Translations, 1948–1968. 2 vols. Boston: G. K. Hall, 1973.

Dardis, Tom. *Firebrand: The Life of Horace Liveright.* New York: Random House, 1995.

Diehl, Carl. *Americans and German Scholarship, 1770–1870.* New Haven, Conn.: Yale University Press, 1978.

Granqvist, Raoul. *Imitation as Resistance: Appropriations of English Literature in Nineteenth-Century America.* Madison, N.J.: Fairleigh Dickinson Press, 1995.

League of Nations [later UNESCO], International Institute of Intellectual Co-operation. *Index Translationum: Répertoire International des Traductions / International Bibliography of Translations.* Paris: League of Nations, 1932– [suspended during World War II].

McLaughlin, Kevin. *Writing in Parts: Imitation and Exchange in Nineteenth-Century Literature.* Stanford, Calif.: Stanford University Press, 1995.

Morgan, Bayard Quincy. *A Critical Bibliography of German Literature in English Translation, 1481–1927.* Second edition. 1938; New York: Scarecrow Press, 1965.

Olmsted, Hugh M. *Translations and Translating: A Selected Bibliography of Bibliographies, Indexes, and Guides.* Binghamton, N.Y.: Center for Translation and Intercultural Communication, 1975.

Pochmann, Henry August. *German Culture in America: Philosophical and Literary Influences, 1600–1900.* Madison: University of Wisconsin Press, 1957.

Vogel, Stanley M. *German Literary Influences on the American Transcendentalists.* 1955; Hamden, Conn.: Archon Books, 1970.

Zboray, Ronald J., and Mary Saracino Zboray. "The Mysteries of New England: Eugène Sue's 'Imitators,' 1844." *Nineteenth-Century Contexts* 22, no. 3 (2000).

n. Serials

American Society of Newspaper Editors, Newspaper History Task Force [Jon Vanden Heuvel]. *Untapped Sources: America's Newspaper Archives and Histories.* Edited by Craig LaMay and Martha FitzSimon. New York: Gannett Foundation Media Center, Columbia University, 1991.

Baldasty, Gerald J. *The Commercialization of News in the Nineteenth Century.* Madison: University of Wisconsin Press, 1992.

Clark, Charles E. *The Public Prints: The Newspaper in Anglo-American Culture, 1665–1740.* New York: Oxford University Press, 1994.

Cloud, Barbara Lee. *The Business of Newspapers on the Western Frontier.* Reno: University of Nevada Press, 1992.

Copeland, David A. *Colonial American Newspapers: Character and Content.* Newark: University of Delaware Press, 1997.

Dicken Garcia, Hazel. *Journalistic Standards in Nineteenth-Century America.* Madison: University of Wisconsin Press, 1989.

Hoerder, Dirk. *The Immigrant Labor Press in North America, 1840s–1970s: An Annotated Bibliography.* 3 vols. New York: Greenwood Press, 1987.

Humphrey, Carol Sue. *The Press of the Young Republic, 1783–1833.* Westport, Conn.: Greenwood Press, 1996.

———. *"This Popular Engine": New England Newspapers during the American Revolution, 1775–1789.* Newark: University of Delaware Press, 1992.

Leonard, Thomas C. *News for All: America's Coming-of-Age with the Press.* New York: Oxford University Press, 1995.

———. *The Power of the Press: The Birth of American Political Reporting.* New York: Oxford University Press, 1986.

Levy, Leonard Williams. *Emergence of a Free Press.* Revised and enlarged edition. New York: Oxford University Press, 1985.

Lewis, Benjamin M. *A Register of Editors, Printers, and Publishers of American Magazines, 1741–1810.* New York: New York Public Library, 1957.

Miller, Sally M. *The Ethnic Press in the United States: A Historical Analysis and Handbook.* New York: Greenwood Press, 1987.

Mott, Frank Luther. *American Journalism: A History, 1690 to 1960.* Third edition. New York: Macmillan, 1962.

———. *A History of American Magazines.* 5 vols. Cambridge: Harvard University Press, 1938–68.

Olasky, Marvin N. *Central Ideas in the Development of American Journalism: A Narrative History.* Hillsdale, N.J.: Lawrence Erlbaum Associates, 1991.

Pratte, Paul Alfred. *Gods within the Machine: A History of the American Society of Newspaper Editors, 1923–1993.* Westport, Conn.: Praeger, 1995.

Price, Kenneth M., and Susan Belasco Smith, eds. *Periodical Literature in Nineteenth-Century America.* Charlottesville: University Press of Virginia, 1995.

———. *Social Texts: Nineteenth-Century American Literature in Periodical Contexts.* Charlottesville: University Press of Virginia, 1995.

Reed, Barbara Straus. *Outsiders in Nineteenth-Century Press History: Multicultural Perspectives.* Bowling Green, Ohio: Bowling Green State University Popular Press, 1995.

Smith, Jeffrey Alan. *Printers and Press Freedom: The Ideology of Early American Journalism.* New York: Oxford University Press, 1988.

Summers, Mark W. *The Press Gang: Newspapers and Politics, 1865–1878.* Chapel Hill: University of North Carolina Press, 1994.

B. PRODUCERS

1. *Writers' Personal and Professional Papers*

NOTE: See Tanselle's Author Lists, *Guide to the Study of United States Imprints,* 162–302.

American Council of Learned Societies. *The Dictionary of American Biography.* 22 vols. New York: C. Scribner's Sons, 1928–58.

Anesko, Michael. *"Friction with the Market": Henry James and the Profession of Authorship.* New York: Oxford University Press, 1986.

Bell, Michael Davitt. "Conditions of Literary Vocation." In *The Cambridge History of American Literature,* vol. 2, *Prose Writing, 1820–1865.* Edited by Sacvan Bercovitch. Cambridge: Cambridge University Press, 1995.

Buell, Lawrence. *New England Literary Culture: From Revolution through Renaissance.* Cambridge: Cambridge University Press, 1986.

Charvat, William. *The Profession of Authorship in America, 1800–1870: The Papers of William Charvat.* Edited by Matthew J. Bruccoli. Columbus: Ohio State University Press, 1968.

Coultrap-McQuin, Susan. *Doing Literary Business: American Women Writers in the Nineteenth Century.* Chapel Hill : University of North Carolina Press, 1990.

Dauber, Kenneth. *The Idea of Authorship in America: Democratic Poetics from Franklin to Melville.* Madison: University of Wisconsin Press, 1990.

Dictionary of Literary Biography. Detroit: Gale Research, 1978–.

Duyckinck, Evert A., and George L. Duyckinck. *Cyclopædia of American Literature.* . . . 2 vols. New York: Charles Scribner, 1855.

Fay, Susan Barrera. "A Modest Celebrity: Literary Reputation and the Marketplace in Antebellum America." Ph.D. diss., George Washington University, 1992.

Fine, Richard. *Hollywood and the Profession of Authorship, 1928–1940.* Ann Arbor, Mich.: UMI Research Press, 1985.

Fink, Steven. *Prophet in the Marketplace: Thoreau's Development as a Professional Writer.* Princeton, N.J.: Princeton University Press, 1992.

Goodrich, Samuel G. *Recollections of a Lifetime; or, Men and Things I Have Seen.* 2 vols. New York: Miller, Orton & Mulligan, 1856.

A Guide to the Harry Ransom Humanities Research Center. Austin: University of Texas, 1990.

Habermas, Jürgen. *The Structural Transformation of the Public Sphere: An Inquiry into a Category of Bourgeois Society.* Translated by Thomas Burger. 1962; Cambridge, Mass.: MIT Press, 1989.

Hamilton, Gail [Mary Abigail Dodge]. *A Battle of the Books, Recorded by an Unknown Writer for the Use of Authors and Publishers.* Cambridge, Mass.: Riverside Press, 1870.

Hemingway, Ernest. *Ernest Hemingway on Writing.* New York: Scribner, 1984.

Henry E. Huntington Library and Art Gallery. *Guide to Literary Manuscripts in the Huntington Library.* San Marino, Calif.: Huntington Library, 1979.

Hinding, Andrea, ed. *Women's History Sources: A Guide to Archives and Manuscript Collections in the United States.* 2 vols. New York: Bowker, 1979.

Index to Personal Names in the National Union Catalog of Manuscript Collections 1959–1984. 2 vols. Alexandria, Va.: Chadwyck-Healey, 1988.

James, Edward, ed. *Notable American Women, 1607–1950.* 3 vols. Cambridge, Mass.: Belknap Press of Harvard University Press, 1971.

Kaenel, Andre. *"Words Are Things": Herman Melville and the Invention of Authorship in Antebellum America.* Bern: P. Lang, 1992.

Kelley, Mary. *Private Woman, Public Stage: Literary Domesticity in Nineteenth-Century America.* New York: Oxford University Press, 1984.

Kingston, Paul William, and Jonathan R. Cole. *The Wages of Writing: Per Word, Per Piece, or Perhaps.* New York: Columbia University Press, 1986.

Kunitz, Stanley J., and Howard Maycraft, eds. *American Authors, 1660–1900: A Biographical Dictionary of American Literature.* New York: H. W. Wilson, 1938.

La Beau, Dennis, ed. *Author Biographies Master Index. . . .* 2 vols. Detroit: Gale Research, 1978.

Leff, Leonard J. *Hemingway and His Conspirators: Hollywood, Scribner's, and the Making of American Celebrity Culture.* Lanham, Md.: Rowman & Littlefield, 1997.

Lentricchia, Frank. "Byron in America: The Later Nineteenth Century." M.A. thesis, Duke University, 1963.

Levy, Andrew. *The Culture and Commerce of the American Short Story.* Cambridge: Cambridge University Press, 1994.

Mainiero, Lina, ed. *American Women Writers: A Critical Reference Guide from Colonial Times to the Present.* 5 vols. New York: Ungar, 1979–94.

McWhirter, David, ed. *Henry James's New York Edition: The Construction of Authorship.* Stanford, Calif.: Stanford University Press, 1995.

Meyers, Jeffrey. *Edmund Wilson: A Biography.* Boston: Houghton Mifflin, 1995.

Miller, Perry. *The Raven and the Whale: The War of Words and Wits in the Era of Poe and Melville.* New York: Harcourt, Brace, 1956.

Modern Language Association of America, Center for Scholarly Editions. *The Center for Scholarly Editions: An Introductory Statement.* New York: Modern Language Association of America, 1977.

National Union Catalog of Manuscript Collections. Washington, D.C.: Library of Congress, 1959–63.

Nelson, Raymond. *Van Wyck Brooks: A Writer's Life.* New York: Dutton, 1981.

Newbury, Michael. *Figuring Authorship in Antebellum America.* Stanford, Calif.: Stanford University Press, 1997.

Paul, Sherman. *Edmund Wilson: A Study of Literary Vocation in Our Time.* Urbana: University of Illinois Press, 1965.

Post-Lauria, Sheila. *Correspondent Colorings: Melville in the Marketplace.* Amherst: University of Massachusetts Press, 1996.

Rasula, Jed. *The American Poetry Wax Musuem: Reality Effects, 1940–1990.* Urbana, Ill.: National Council of Teachers of English, 1996.

Renker, Elizabeth. *Strike through the Mask: Herman Melville and the Scene of Writing.* Baltimore: Johns Hopkins University Press, 1996.

Rice, Grantland S. *The Transformation of Authorship in America.* Chicago: University of Chicago Press, 1997.

Rice, William Craig. *Public Discourse and Academic Inquiry.* New York: Garland, 1996.

Robbins, J. Albert. *American Literary Manuscripts: A Checklist of Holdings in Academic, Historical, and Public Libraries, Museums, and Authors' Homes in the United States.* Second edition. New York: American Literature Section, Modern Language Association, 1977.

Rowland, William G., Jr. *Literature and the Marketplace: Romantic Writers and Their Audiences in Great Britain and the United States.* Lincoln: University of Nebraska Press, 1996.

Shields, David S. *Civil Tongues and Polite Letters in British America.* Chapel Hill: University of North Carolina Press, 1997.

Sicherman, Barbara, and Carol Hurd Green, eds. *Notable American Women: The Modern Period.* Cambridge, Mass.: Belknap Press of Harvard University Press, 1980.

Spencer, Benjamin Townley. *The Quest for Nationality: An American Literary Campaign.* Syracuse, N.Y.: Syracuse University Press, 1957.

Szladits, Lola L. *Perennials: A Fiftieth Anniversary Selection from the Berg Collection.* New York: New York Public Library, 1988.

Tweedie, F. J., S. Singh, and D. I. Holmes. "Neural Network Applications in Stylometry: The Federalist Papers." *Computers and the Humanities* [Netherlands] 30 (1996): 1–10.

Wallace, James D. *Early Cooper and His Audience.* New York: Columbia University Press, 1986.

Warner, Michael. *The Letters of the Republic: Publication and the Public Sphere in Eighteenth-Century America.* Cambridge, Mass.: Harvard University Press, 1990.

Watts, Steven. *The Romance of Real Life: Charles Brockden Brown and the Origins of American Culture.* Baltimore: Johns Hopkins University Press, 1994.

Weber, Ronald. *Hired Pens: Professional Writers in America's Golden Age of Print.* Athens: Ohio University Press, 1997.

West, James L., III. *American Authors and the Literary Marketplace since 1900.* Philadelphia: University of Pennsylvania Press, 1988.

White, Luke, Jr. *Henry William Herbert and the American Publishing Scene, 1831–1858.* Newark, N. J.: Carteret Book Club, 1943.

Wilson, Christopher P. *The Labor of Words: Literary Professionalism in the Progressive Era.* Athens: University of Georgia Press, 1985.

Wilson, James Grant, and John Fiske, eds. *Appleton's Cyclopedia of American Biography.* 6 vols. New York: D. Appleton, 1887–89.

Zboray, Ronald J. "Books." In *Handbook on Mass Media in the United States: The Industry and Its Audiences.* Edited by Erwin K. Thomas and Brown M. Carpenter. Westport, Conn.: Greenwood Press, 1994.

———. "Cheap Publishing in Antebellum Boston: John Townsend Trowbridge's *Martin Merrivale: His 'X' Mark.*" *Dime Novel Round-up* 60 (October 1992): 78–83.

2. *Literary Agents*

Brown, James Oliver. "My Life as a Literary Agent." *Columbia Library Columns* 39 (February 1990): 11–21.

Christopher, Joe R. "Sayers and Her Literary Agent: Dorothy L. Sayers' Correspondence with Her Agent, 1950, An Annotated Checklist." *Sidelights on Sayers* 43 (July 1995): 10–14.

Curtis, Richard. *Beyond the Bestseller: A Literary Agent Takes You inside the Book Business.* New York: New American Library, 1989.

Fitzgerald, F. Scott. *As Ever, Scott Fitz—; Letters between F. Scott Fitzgerald and His Literary Agent Harold Ober, 1919–1940.* Edited by Matthew J. Bruccoli. Philadelphia: Lippincott, 1972.

Jackinson, Alex. *The Barnum-Cinderella World of Publishing.* New York: Impact, 1971.

———. *The Romance of Publishing: An Agent Recalls Thirty-Three Years with Authors and Editors.* New York: Cornwall Books, 1987.

Thomson, Christine Campbell. *I Am a Literary Agent: Memories Personal and Professional.* London: S. Low, Marston, 1951.

Wolfe, Thomas. *Beyond Love and Loyalty: The Letters of Thomas Wolfe and Elizabeth Nowell.* Edited by Richard S. Kennedy. Chapel Hill: University of North Carolina Press, 1983.

3. *Publishers*

NOTE: See several of the sources listed in section I. Introduction: Charvat, *Literary Publishing in America*; Lehmann-Haupt and others, *The Book in*

America; McMurtrie, *A History of Printing in the United States*; Tebbel, *A History of Book Publishing in the United States*; Thomas, *A History of Printing in America*; Zboray, *A Fictive People*.

Advertiser's Gazette. New York: G. P. Rowell & Co., 1866–76[?].

American Newspaper Publishers Association, Bureau of Advertising. *National Advertising Expenditures by Classification in Newspapers, Magazines, Chain Radio, Farm Journals*. 4 vols. New York: American Newspaper Publishers Association, 1930, 1938.

American Newspaper Reporter and Printers Gazette. New York: G. P. Rowell & Co., 1871–76.

Archives of Harper & Brothers, 1817–1914. [Microform.] Cambridge: Chadwyck-Healey, 1980.

Ashley, Perry J., ed. *American Newspaper Publishers, 1950–1990*. Detroit: Gale Research, 1993.

Bartlett, Lee. *Kenneth Rexroth and James Laughlin: Selected Letters*. New York: W. W. Norton, 1991.

Basford, Harry Miller. *How to Advertise Printing*. New York: Oswald, 1915.

Berg, A. Scott. *Max Perkins, Editor of Genius*. New York: Dutton, 1978.

Bernard, Andre. *Rotten Rejections: A Literary Companion*. Wainscott, N.Y.: Pushcart Press, 1990.

Bruccoli, Matthew J., ed. *The Only Thing That Counts: The Ernest Hemingway/Maxwell Perkins Correspondence, 1925–1947*. New York: Scribner, 1996.

Canning, Peter. *American Dreamers: The Wallaces and Reader's Digest: An Insider's Story*. New York: Simon & Schuster, 1996.

Cerf, Bennett. *At Random: The Reminiscences of Bennett Cerf*. New York: Random House, 1977.

Charvat, William. "James T. Fields and the Beginnings of Book Promotion." *Huntington Library Quarterly* 8 (1944): 82–94.

Commins, Dorothy. *"Love and Admiration and Respect": The O'Neill-Commins Correspondence*. Durham, N.C.: Duke University Press, 1986.

———. *What Is an Editor? Saxe Commins at Work*. Chicago: University of Chicago Press, 1978.

Coser, Lewis A., Charles Kadushin, and Walter W. Powell. *Books: The Culture and Commerce of Publishing*. New York: Basic Books, 1982.

Cowley, Malcolm. *Unshaken Friend: A Profile of Maxwell Perkins*. Boulder, Colo.: R. Rinehart, 1985.

Curtis Publishing Co. *Advertising in* Ladies' Home Journal *and Other Women's Publications.* Philadelphia: Curtis, 1926.

Derby, James Cephas. *Fifty Years among Authors, Books and Publishers.* New York: Carleton, 1884.

Doubleday, Frank Nelson. *The Memoirs of a Publisher.* Garden City, N.Y.: Doubleday, 1972.

Drinkwater, John. *A Book for Bookmen: Being Edited Manuscripts and Marginalia with Essays on Several Occasions.* London: Dulau, 1926.

Dzwonkoski, Peter, ed. *American Literary Publishing Houses, 1639–1899 and 1900–1980: Trade and Paperback.* Detroit, Mich.: Gale Research, 1986.

Eidesheim, Julie. *Editor at Work.* New York: Farrar & Rinehart, 1939.

Exman, Eugene. *Brothers Harper: A Unique Publishing Partnership and Its Impact upon the Cultural Life of America from 1817 to 1853.* New York: Harper & Row, 1965.

Faulkner, William. *As I Lay Dying: Holograph Manuscript and Carbon Typescript.* Introduced and arranged by Thomas L. McHaney. New York: Garland, 1987.

Feather, John. *English Book Prospectuses: An Illustrated History.* Newtown, Pa.: Bird & Bull Press, 1984.

Fensch, Thomas, ed. *Steinbeck and Covici: The Story of a Friendship.* Middlebury, Vt.: P. S. Eriksson, 1979.

Fitzgerald, F. Scott. *The Great Gatsby: The Revised and Rewritten Galleys.* Edited by Matthew J. Bruccoli. New York: Garland, 1990.

Fragasso, Philip M. "John P. Jewett: The Unsung Hero of *Uncle Tom's Cabin.*" *New England Galaxy* 20 (Summer 1978): 22–29.

Gaskell, Philip. *From Writer to Reader: Studies in Editorial Method.* Oxford: Clarendon Press of Oxford University Press, 1978.

Geary, Susan. "Harriet Beecher Stowe, John P. Jewett, and Author-Publisher Relations in 1853." *Studies in the American Renaissance* 1 (1977): 345–67.

Gordon, David M. *Ezra Pound and James Laughlin: Selected Letters.* New York: W. W. Norton, 1994.

Graham, Katharine. *Personal History.* New York: A. A. Knopf, 1997.

Gross, Gerald, ed. *Editors on Editing.* New York: Grosset & Dunlap, 1962.

Henderson, Bill. *The Art of Literary Publishing: Editors on Their Craft.* Yonkers, N.Y.: Pushcart, 1980.

Highton, Albert H. *Practical Proofreading.* Chicago: Department of Education, United Typothetae of America, 1926.

Hill, Frank Ernest. *Reminiscences of Frank Ernest Hill.* Glen Rock, N.J.: Microfilming Corporation of America, 1972.

Horne, Philip. *Henry James and Revision: The New York Edition.* Oxford: Clarendon Press of Oxford University Press, 1990.

Hungerford, Herbert. *How Publishers Win: A Case Record Commentary on Personal Experiences and Interviews with Prominent Publishers Showing How Books and Periodicals Are Made and Marketed.* Washington, D.C.: Ransdell, 1931.

James, Henry. *The Correspondence of Henry James and the House of Macmillan, 1877–1914: "All the links in the Chain."* Edited by Rayburn S. Moore. Baton Rouge: Louisiana State University Press, 1993.

Langford, Gerald. *Faulkner's Revision of* Sanctuary: *A Collation of the Unrevised Galleys and the Published Book.* Austin: University of Texas Press, 1972.

Luey, Beth, and others. *A Guide to Book Publishers' Archives.* New York: Book Industry Study Group, 1996.

MacGregor, Frank. *Reminiscences of Frank MacGregor.* Glen Rock, N.J.: Microfilming Corporation of America, 1977.

Moore, John Hammond. *Wiley, One Hundred and Seventy Five Years of Publishing.* New York: Wiley, 1982.

National Advertising Records. . . . New York: Denney, 1928–33.

Neuharth, Allen. *Confessions of an S.O.B.* New York: Doubleday, 1989.

PIB: Magazine Service. South Norwalk, Conn.: Leading National Advertisers, 1949.

Pound, Ezra. *Pound/the* Little Review: *The Letters of Ezra Pound to Margaret Anderson: The* Little Review *Correspondence.* Edited by Thomas L. Scott and others. New York: New Directions, 1988.

Publishers Information Bureau. *National Advertising Records.* New York: Publishers Information Bureau, 1936–[?].

Remer, Rosalind. *Printers and Men of Capital: Philadelphia Book Publishers in the New Republic.* Philadelphia: University of Pennsylvania Press, 1996.

Ross, Charles L., and Dennis Jackson, eds. *Editing D. H. Lawrence: New Versions of a Modern Author.* Ann Arbor: University of Michigan Press, 1995.

Scanlon, Jennifer. *Inarticulate Longings: The* Ladies' Home Journal, *Gender, and the Promises of Consumer Culture.* New York: Routledge, 1995.

Scribner, Charles. *In the Company of Writers: A Life in Publishing.* New York: Scribner, 1990.

Simpson, Percy. *Proof-Reading in the Sixteenth, Seventeenth, and Eighteenth Centuries.* London: Oxford University Press, 1935.

Stainton, Elsie Myers. *Author and Editor at Work: Making a Better Book.* Toronto: University of Toronto Press, 1982.

Stern, Madeleine B. *Books and Book People in Nineteenth-Century America.* New York: Bowker, 1978.

————. *Imprints on History: Book Publishers and American Frontiers.* Bloomington: Indiana University Press, 1956.

Stern, Madeleine B., ed. *Publishers for Mass Entertainment in Nineteenth-Century America.* Boston: G. K. Hall, 1980.

Tryon, Warren S. *Parnassus Corner: A Life of James T. Fields, Publisher to the Victorians.* Boston: Houghton Mifflin, 1963.

Tryon, Warren S., and William Charvat, eds. *The Cost Books of Ticknor & Fields and Their Predecessors, 1832–1858.* New York: Bibliographical Society of America, 1949.

Uhlan, Edward. *The Rogue of Publishers' Row: Confessions of a Publisher.* New York: Exposition Press, 1956.

Winship, Michael. *American Literary Publishing in the Mid-Nineteenth Century: The Business of Ticknor & Fields.* Cambridge: Cambridge University Press, 1995.

Zboray, Ronald J. "Literary Enterprise and the Mass Market: Publishing and Business Innovation in Antebellum America." *Essays in Economic and Business History* 10 (1992): 168–81.

4. Printers

American Printers Specimen Exchange. *Specimens of Handwork by Printers in All Parts of America and Many Foreign Countries.* Buffalo: Ed. H. McClure, 1888.

Angelo, Valenti. *Valenti Angelo: Author, Illustrator, Printer, An Autobiographical Story.* Bronxville, N.Y.: V. Angelo, 1971[?].

Baker, Elizabeth Faulkner. *Displacement of Men by Machines: Effects of Technological Change in Commercial Printing.* New York: Columbia University Press, 1933.

————. *Printers and Technology: A History of the International Printing Pressmen and Assistants' Union.* New York: Columbia University Press, 1957.

Baron, Ava. "Woman's 'Place' in Capitalist Production: A Study of Class Relations in the Nineteenth Century Newspaper Printing Industry." Ph.D. diss., New York University, 1981.

Bliss, Carey S., ed. *A Pair on Printing: Atkyns' The Original and Growth of Printing, William Caslon and the First English Type Specimen Book.* North Hills, Pa.: Bird & Bull Press, 1982.

Blumenthal, Joseph. *Typographic Years: A Printer's Journey through a Half-Century, 1925–1975.* New York: F. C. Beil, 1982.

Bruckner, D. J. R. *Frederic Goudy.* New York: Documents of American Design, H. N. Abrams, 1978.

Buckingham, Joseph T. *Personal Memoirs and Recollections of Editorial Life.* 2 vols. Boston: Ticknor, Reed & Fields, 1852.

Cockburn, Cynthia. *Brothers: Male Dominance and Technological Change.* London: Pluto Press, 1983.

De Vinne, Theodore Low. *The Printers' Price List; A Manual for the Use of Clerks and Book-Keepers in Job Printing Offices.* New York: Francis Hart, 1869.

Dickinson, Samuel Nelson. *A Help to Printers and Publishers. . . .* Boston: S. N. Dickinson, 1835.

Dyer, Alan. *A Biography of James Parker, Colonial Printer.* Troy, N.Y.: Whitson Publishing, 1982.

Ford, Paul Leicester, ed. *The Journals of Hugh Gaine, Printer.* 2 vols. New York: Dodd, Mead, 1902.

Franklin Typographical Society. *Constitution and Catalogue of the Library of the Franklin Typographical Society.* Boston: Snow & White, 1850.

Gaskell, Philip, Giles Barber, and Georgina Warrilow. "An Annotated List of Printers' Manuals to 1850." *Journal of the Printing History Society* 4 (1968): 11–32.

Grabhorn, Jane Bisell. *Thanks, Jane: Jane Bisell Grabhorn, 1911–1973.* Oakland, Calif.: Rather Press, 1974.

Gray, Nicolete. *Nineteenth-Century Ornamented Typefaces.* Berkeley: University of California Press, 1976.

Green, Ralph. *A Check List of American Nineteenth Century Type Specimen Books.* Chicago: Green, 1951.

Gress, Edmund G. *The American Handbook of Printing, Containing in Brief and Simple Style Something about Every Department of the Art and Business of Printing.* New York: Oswald, 1907.

———. *The Art and Practice of Typography. . . .* New York: Oswald [later Harper], 1910–31.

Hamilton, Milton W. *The Country Printer: New York State, 1785–1830.* New York: Columbia University Press, 1936.

Heartman, Charles F. *Checklist of Printers in the United States from Stephen Daye to the Close of the War of Independence*. New York: private printing, 1915.

Holtzberg-Call, Maggie. *The Lost World of the Craft Printer*. Urbana: University of Illinois Press, 1992.

Johnson, Foster Macy. *The Typographical Resources of a Country Printer*. Meriden, Conn.: Bayberry Hill Press, 1959.

Levenson, Roger. *Women in Printing: Northern California, 1857–1890: Including a Roster of Women and a Checklist of Imprints*. Santa Barbara: Capra Press, 1994.

Lipset, Seymour Martin, Martin A. Trow, and James S. Coleman. *Union Democracy: The Internal Politics of the International Typographical Union*. Glencoe, Ill.: Free Press, 1956.

Lynch, Thomas. *The Printer's Manual: A Practical Guide for Compositors and Pressmen*. Second edition. Cincinnati: Cincinnati Type Foundry, 1864.

MacKellar, Thomas. *The American Printer: A Manual of Typography*. Second edition. Philadelphia: MacKellar, Smiths & Jordan, 1866–93.

McKitterick, David, ed. *Stanley Morison and D. B. Updike: Selected Correspondence*. New York: Moretus Press, 1979.

McMurtrie, Douglas, ed. *Letters of Peter Timothy*. Chicago: Black Cat Press, 1935.

McVicar, John. *Origin and Progress of the Typographical Union: Its Proceedings as National and International Organization, 1850–1891*. Lansing, Mich.: Thorp, 1891.

Mumey, Nolie, ed. *Nathan Addison Baker, 1843–1934: Pioneer Journalist, Teacher, Printer, Agriculturalist, Real Estate Dealer, Stockman, Founder of Early Journalism in Wyoming, and a Distinguished Citizen: His Diary of 1865, 1866, 1867*. Denver: Old West Publishing, 1965.

Naas, Bernard G., and Carmelita Sakr. *American Labor Union Periodicals: A Guide to Their Location*. Ithaca, N.Y.: Cornell University, 1956.

Oswald, John Clyde. *A History of Printing: Its Development through Five Hundred Years*. New York: Appleton, 1928.

Porte, R. T. *How to Figure Costs in Printing Offices*. Minneapolis: Minnesota Cost System, 1914.

Printers' Free Library. *Catalogue of the Printers' Library*. New York: Printers' Free Library, 1852.

Rather, Lois. *Henry George—Printer to Author*. Oakland, Calif.: Rather Press, 1978.

Reynolds, Lloyd G., and Charles C. Killingsworth. *Trade Union Publications: The Official Journals, Convention Proceedings, and Constitutions of International Unions and Federations, 1850–1941.* 3 vols. Baltimore: Johns Hopkins University Press, 1944–45.

Rorabaugh, William J. *The Craft Apprentice from Franklin to the Machine Age in America.* New York: Oxford University Press, 1986.

Rosemont, Henry P. "Benjamin Franklin and the Philadelphia Typographical Strike of 1786." *Labor History* 22 (1981): 398–421.

Silver, Rollo G. "Abstracts from the Wills and Estates of Boston Printers, 1800–1825." *Studies in Bibliography* 7 (1955): 212–18.

———. *The American Printer, 1787–1825.* Charlottesville: University Press of Virginia, 1967.

———. *Benjamin Edes, Trumpeter of Sedition.* New York: Bibliographical Society of America, 1953.

Stewart, Ethelbert. *A Documentary History of the Early Organizations of Printers.* Washington, D.C.: Government Printing Office, 1905.

Tracy, George A., ed. *History of the Typographical Union. . . .* Indianapolis: International Typographical Union, 1913.

Typophiles. *Theodore Low De Vinne.* 2 vols. New York: Typophiles, 1968.

United Typothetae of America. *U.T.A. Simplified Cost Finding System. . . .* Washington, D.C.: Typothetae, 1934.

Van Winkle, C. S. *The Printer's Guide, or An Introduction to the Art of Printing: Including an Essay on Punctuation and Remarks on Orthography.* New York: Van Winkle, 1818.

Wroth, Lawrence C. *Benjamin Franklin, Printer at Work. . . .* New York: private printing, 1974.

———. *The Colonial Printer.* 1931; Portland, Me.: Southworth-Anthoensen Press, 1938.

———. "Corpus Typographicum: A Review of English and American Printers' Manuals." *Dolphin* 2 (1935): 157–70.

Zeitlin and Ver Brugge. *The Library of a California Printer. . . .* Los Angeles: Zeitlin and Ver Brugge, 1950.

5. Other

Annenberg, Maurice. *Type Foundries of America and Their Catalogs.* New Castle, Del.: Oak Knoll Press, 1994.

Badaracco, Claire Hoertz. *Trading Words: Poetry, Typography, and Illustrated Books in the Modern Literary Economy.* Baltimore: Johns Hopkins University Press, 1995.

Baker, William Spohn. *American Engravers and Their Works*. Philadelphia: Gebbie & Barrie, 1875.

Boger, Astrid. *Documenting Lives: James Agee's and Walker Evans's Let Us Now Praise Famous Men*. Frankfurt am Main: P. Lang, 1994.

Bolton, Theodore. *American Book Illustrators: Bibliographic Checklist of 123 Artists*. New York: R. R. Bowker, 1938.

Brenni, Vito J. *Bookbinding: A Guide to the Literature*. Westport, Conn.: Greenwood Press, 1982.

———. *Book Illustration and Decoration: A Guide to Research*. Westport, Conn.: Greenwood Press, 1980.

Brown, H. Glenn, and Maude O. Brown. *A Directory of the Book-Arts and Book Trade in Philadelphia to 1820 Including Painters and Engravers*. New York: New York Public Library, 1950.

Bruce, David. *The History of Typefounding in the United States*. New York: Typophiles, 1981.

Comparato, Frank E. *Books for the Millions: A History of the Men Whose Methods and Machines Packaged the Printed Word*. Harrisburg, Pa.: Stackpole, 1971.

———. *Chronicles of Genius and Folly: R. Hoe & Company and the Printing Press as a Service to Democracy*. Culver City, Calif.: Labyrinthos, 1979.

Darton, F. J. Harvey. *Modern Book-Illustration in Great Britain and America*. London: Studio Limited, 1931.

De Vinne, Theodore Low. *The Practice of Typography*. . . . 4 vols. New York: Century, 1900–1904.

Fisher, Paul Leslie, Jr. "Modernism in American Typography, 1925–1934." Ph.D. diss., Columbia University, 1950.

French, Hannah D. *Bookbinding in Early America: Seven Essays on Masters and Methods*. Worcester, Mass.: American Antiquarian Society, 1986.

Groce, George C., and David Wallace. *The New-York Historical Society's Dictionary of Artists in America, 1564–1860*. New Haven: Yale University Press, 1957.

Hamilton, Sinclair. *Early American Book Illustrators and Wood Engravers, 1670–1870*. . . . Princeton, N. J.: Princeton University Press, 1958.

Hunter, Dard. *Papermaking: The History and Technique of an Ancient Craft*. Second edition. New York: Alfred A. Knopf, 1947.

International Brotherhood of Bookbinders. *The International Bookbinder*. Washington, D.C.: J. L. Feeney, 1900–1972.

Johnson, Mary-Parke. "An Inventory of the Joseph T. Altemus Book Bindery, Philadelphia, 1854." *Papers of the Bibliographical Society of America* 80 (1986): 179–91.

Kelly, Rob Roy. *American Wood Type, 1828–1900.* . . . New York: Van Nostrand Reinhold, 1969.

Lehmann-Haupt, Hellmut, Hannah D. French, and Joseph W. Rogers. *Bookbinding in America: Three Essays.* . . . 1941; New York: R. R. Bowker, 1967.

Levarie, Norma. *The Art and History of Books.* 1982; New Castle, Del.: Oak Knoll Press, 1994.

Linton, W. J. *The History of Wood-Engraving in America.* Boston: Estes & Lauriat, 1882.

Loring, Rosamond. *Decorated Book Papers: Being an Account of Their Designs and Fashions.* Cambridge, Mass.: Harvard College Library, 1942, 1952.

McGaw, Judith A. *Most Wonderful Machine: Mechanization and Social Change in Berkshire Paper Making, 1801–1885.* Princeton, N.J.: Princeton University Press, 1987.

McGrath, Daniel F. "American Colorplate Books, 1800–1900." Ph.D. diss., University of Michigan, 1966.

McGrew, Mac. *American Metal Typefaces of the Twentieth Century.* Second revised edition. New Castle, Del.: Oak Knoll Books, 1993.

Pomeroy, Jane R. "On the Changes Made in Wood Engravings in the Stereotyping Process." *Printing History* 17 (1995): 35–40.

Silver, Rollo. "'The Flash of the Comet': The Typographical Career of Samuel N. Dickinson." *Studies in Bibliography* 31 (1978): 68–89.

———. *Typefounding in America, 1787–1825.* Charlottesville: University Press of Virginia, 1965.

Stauffer, David M., and others. *American Engravers upon Copper and Steel.* 3 vols. 1907; New Castle, Del.: Oak Knoll Books, 1994.

Weitenkampf, Frank. *The Illustrated Book.* Cambridge, Mass.: Harvard University Press, 1938.

6. Books as Artifactual and Documentary Evidence

Bowers, Fredson. *Bibliography and Textual Criticism.* Oxford: Clarendon Press, 1964.

———. *Principles of Bibliographic Description.* Princeton, N.J.: Princeton University Press, 1949.

Duncan, Harry. *Doors of Perception: Essays in Book Typography.* Austin, Tex.: W. Thomas Taylor, 1983.

Gaskell, Philip. *A New Introduction to Bibliography.* New York: Oxford University Press, 1972.

Greg, Walter Wilson. *Bibliography of the English Printed Drama to the Restoration*. 4 vols. London: Bibliographical Society, 1939–59.

———. *The Editorial Problem in Shakespeare*. Third edition. Oxford: Clarendon Press, 1954.

McKenzie, D. F. *Bibliography and the Sociology of Texts*. [The Panizzi Lectures, 1985.] London: British Library, 1986.

McKerrow, Ronald B. *An Introduction to Bibliography for Literary Students*. Winchester: St Paul's Bibliographies, 1994.

Stoddard, Roger E. *Marks in Books, Illustrated and Explained*. Cambridge, Mass.: Houghton Library, Harvard University, 1985.

Tanselle, G. Thomas. *A Description of Descriptive Bibliography*. Washington, D.C.: Library of Congress, 1992.

7. Books and the Law

Benjamin, Curtis G. *U.S. Books Abroad: Neglected Ambassadors*. Washington, D.C.: Library of Congress, 1984.

Bennett, James R. *Control of Information in the United States: An Annotated Bibliography*. Westport, Conn.: Meckler Corp., 1987.

Butler, Pierce. *Books and Libraries in Wartime*. Chicago: University of Chicago Press, 1945.

Chafee, Zechariah. *Free Speech in the United States*. Cambridge, Mass.: Harvard University Press, 1941.

Cole, John Y. "Of Copyright, Men, and a National Library." *Quarterly Journal of the Library of Congress* 28 (April 1971): 114–36.

Foerstel, Herbert N. *Free Expression and Censorship in America: An Encyclopedia*. Westport, Conn.: Greenwood Press, 1997.

Gilreath, James, ed. *Federal Copyright Records, 1790–1800*. Elizabeth Carter Wills, comp. Washington, D.C.: Library of Congress, 1987.

Gordon, George Stuart. *Anglo-American Literary Relations*. London: Oxford University Press, 1942.

Hoffman, Frank W. *Intellectual Freedom and Censorship: An Annotated Bibliography*. Metuchen, N.J.: Scarecrow Press, 1989.

Hurwitz, Leon. *Historical Dictionary of Censorship in the United States*. Westport, Conn.: Greenwood Press, 1985.

Kraus, H. P. *Inter-American and World Book Trade: Problems of Organization*. New York: private printing, 1944.

Mitgang, Herbert. *Dangerous Dossiers: Exposing the Secret War against America's Greatest Authors*. New York: D. I. Fine, 1988.

Rosenbloom, Joshua L. "Economics and the Emergence of Modern Publishing in the United States." *Publishing History* 29 (1991): 47–68.

Schroeder, Theodore. *Free Speech Bibliography. . . .* New York: H. W. Wilson, 1922.

Tanselle, G. Thomas. "Copyright Records and the Bibliographer." *Studies in Bibliography* 22 (1969): 77–124.

U.S. Copyright Office. *Catalogue of Copyright Entries.* Washington, D.C.: Government Printing Office, July 1906–.

———. *Catalogue of Title-Entries.* 47 vols. Washington, D.C.: Government Printing Office, 1 July 1891–June 1906.

———. *Copyright Enactment: Laws Passed in the United States since 1783 Relating to Copyright.* Washington, D.C.: Government Printing Office, 1900, 1963.

C. DISSEMINATORS

1. *Distributors*

American News Company. *Covering a Continent: A Story of Newsstand Distribution and Sales.* New York: American News, 1930.

———. *Serving the Reading Public: America's Leading Distributor of Books, Magazines, and Newspapers Celebrates 80 Years of Growth.* New York: American News, 1944.

Arthur Andersen & Co. *Book Distribution in the United States: Issues and Perceptions.* New York: Book Industry Study Group, 1982.

Cooper, Kent. *Barriers Down: The Story of the News Agency Epoch.* New York: Farrar & Rinehart, 1942.

Hackenberg, Michael, ed. *Getting the Books Out: Papers of the Chicago Conference on the Book in Nineteenth-Century America.* Washington, D.C.: Center for the Book, Library of Congress, 1987.

Schurman, Lydia Cushman. "Those Famous American Periodicals—The Bible, the Odyssey and Paradise Lost—Or, The Great Second-Class Mail Swindle." *Publishing History* [Great Britain] 40 (1996): 33–52.

Zboray, Ronald J. "The Transportation Revolution and Antebellum Book Distribution Reconsidered." *American Quarterly* 38 (1986): 53–71.

2. *Retailers*

Alger, Horatio, Jr. *The Young Book Agent; or, Frank Hardy's Road to Success.* New York: Street & Smith, 1906.

American Booksellers' Guide. New York: American News, 1868–75.

American Book Trade Manual. 3 vols. New York: R. R. Bowker, 1915–22.

Amory, Hugh. "Under the Exchange: The Unprofitable Business of Michael Perry, a Seventeenth-Century Boston Bookseller." *Proceedings of the American Antiquarian Society* 103, pt. 1 (1993): 31–60.

Andersen, Charles B. *Bookselling in America and the World: Some Observations & Recollections in Celebration of the 75th Anniversary of the American Booksellers Association.* New York: Quadrangle, 1975.

Andersen, Charles B., and G. Roysce Smith, eds. *A Manual on Bookselling: How to Open and Run Your Own Bookstore.* New York: Harmony Books, 1974.

Arbour, Keith. *Canvassing Books, Sample Books, and Subscription Publishers' Ephemera, 1833–1951 in the Collection of Michael Zinman.* Ardsley, N.Y.: Haydn Foundation for the Cultural Arts, 1996.

Atherton, Lewis. *The Frontier Merchant in Mid-America.* Columbia: University of Missouri Press, 1971.

———. *The Southern Country Store, 1800–1860.* Baton Rouge: Louisiana State University Press, 1949.

Bosse, David. "A Canvasser's Tale." *Map Collector* [Great Britain] 57 (1991): 22–26.

Boynton, Henry Walcott. *Annals of American Bookselling, 1638–1850.* 1932; New Castle, Del.: Oak Knoll, 1991.

Brigham, Clarence S. "American Booksellers' Catalogues, 1734–1800." In *Essays Honoring Lawrence C. Wroth.* Portland, Me.: Anthoensen Press, 1951.

Butler, Ellis Parker. *Dollarature; or, The Drug-Store Book.* Boston: Houghton Mifflin, 1930.

Caspar, C. N. *Caspar's Directory of the American Book, News and Stationery Trade, Wholesale and Retail. . . .* Milwaukee: C. N. Caspar, 1889.

Cody, Pat, and Fred Cody. *Cody's Books: The Life and Times of a Berkeley Bookstore, 1956–1977.* San Francisco: Chronicle Books, 1992.

Dumond, Annie. *Annie Nelles; or, The Life of a Book Agent: An Autobiography.* Cincinnati: A. Nelles, 1868.

Dutton, E. P. *Seventy-Five Years; or, The Joys and Sorrows of Selling Books at Duttons, from 1852 to 1927.* New York: Duttons, 1927.

Garnett, David. *Never Be a Bookseller.* New York: Knopf, 1929.

Graham, Bessie. *The Bookman's Manual: A Guide to Literature.* New York: R. R. Bowker, 1924.

Green, James N. "'The Cowl Knows Best What Will Suit in Virginia': Parson Weems on Southern Readers." *Printing History* 17 (1995): 26–34.

Gross, Sidney, and Phyllis B. Steckler, eds. *How to Run a Paperback Bookshop.* New York: R. R. Bowker, 1963.

Growoll, Adolf. *American Book Clubs: Their Beginnings and History, and a Bibliography of Their Publications.* New York: Dodd, Mead, 1897.

————. *The Booksellers' League: A History of Its Formation and Ten Years of Its Work.* New York: The Booksellers' League, 1905.

————. *A Booksellers's Library and How to Use It.* New York: Publisher's Weekly, 1891.

————. *The Profession of Bookselling: A Handbook of Practical Hints for the Apprentice and Bookseller.* 3 vols. New York: Office of the Publishers' Weekly, 1893–1913.

Hard, Margaret. *A Memory of Vermont: Our Life in the Johnny Appleseed Bookshop, 1930–1965.* New York: Harcourt, Brace & World, 1967.

Harrington, Bates. *How 'Tis Done: A Thorough Ventilation of the Numerous Schemes Conducted by Wandering Canvassers. . . .* Chicago: Fidelity Publishing, 1879.

Harris, Susan K. *The Courtship of Olivia Langdon and Mark Twain.* Cambridge: Cambridge University Press, 1996.

Jaffee, David. "Peddlers of Progress and the Transformation of the Rural North, 1760–1860." *Journal of American History* 78 (1991): 511–35.

Jenison, Madge. *Sunwise Turn: A Human Comedy of Bookselling.* New York: E. P. Dutton, 1923.

Jumonville, Florence M. "Books, Libraries, and Undersides for the Skies of Beds: The Extraordinary Career of A. L. Boimare." *Louisiana History* 34 (1993): 437–59.

Kroch, Adolph. *A Great Bookstore in Action.* Chicago: University of Chicago Press, 1940.

Leacock, Stephen. *The Methods of Mr. Sellyer: A Book Store Study.* New York: John Lane, 1914.

Likins, Mrs. J. W. *Six Years Experience as a Book Agent in California, including My Trip from New York to San Francisco via Nicaragua.* 1874; San Francisco: Book Club of San Francisco, 1992.

Link, Henry C., and Harry Arthur Hopf. *People and Books: A Study of Reading and Book-Buying Habits.* New York: Book Industry Committee, Book Manufacturers' Institute, 1946.

Lowman, Al. "The Life and Death of a Bookstore." *Southwestern Historical Quarterly* 91 (1987): 173–84.

Luthy, David. "A History of Raber's Bookstore." *Mennonite Quarterly Review* 58 (1984): 168–78.

Melcher, Frederic G. *The Successful Bookshop.* New York: National Association of Book Publishers, 1928.

Naumberg, Edward, Jr. "My Favorite Bookseller." *Princeton University Library Chronicle* 48 (1987): 181–90.

Nicely, Tom. "J. Francis Ruggles, Ye Bibliopoloexperto of Bronson." *American Magazine and Historical Chronicle* 3 (1987): 16–27.

Norris, Joe L. *Pioneer Marketing Associations of the American Book Trade, 1873–1901.* Chicago: private printing, 1941.

Noyes, Henry. *China Born: Adventures of a Maverick Bookman.* San Francisco: China Books & Periodicals, 1989.

Park, Ruth Brown. *Book Shops, How to Run Them.* Garden City, N.Y.: Doubleday, Doran Book Shops, 1929.

Powell, Walter W. "Whither the Local Bookstore?" *Daedalus* 112 (1983): 51–64.

Radway, Janice A. *A Feeling for Books: The Book-of-the-Month Club, Literary Taste, and Middle-Class Desire.* Chapel Hill: University of North Carolina Press, 1997.

Rohleder, Charles A. *The Newspaper Boy: Merchant or Employee?* Indianapolis: Newspaper Boys of America, 1937.

Sargent, George S. *The Book Catalogue and How It Should Be Printed.* Portland, Me.: Southworth Press, 1924.

Schwartz, Harry W. *Fifty Years in My Bookstore: or, A Life with Books.* Milwaukee: Schwartz, 1977.

Sorel, Paul. *Establishing and Operating a Book Store.* Washington, D.C.: U.S. Government Printing Office, 1946.

Stafford, Marjorie. "Subscription Book Publishing in the United States, 1865–1930." M.A. thesis, University of Illinois, 1943.

Starr, George Washington. *Operating Results of College Bookstores.* Bloomington: Indiana University School of Business Research, 1939.

Storke, Elliot G. *Sample Subscription Book of the Great American Rebellion,* vol. 2, *Containing the Style of Binding and the Breadth of Back of That Volume, and Full Specimens of the Third and Fourth Parts of the Work.* Auburn, N.Y.: Auburn Publishing, 1863.

United States Literary Advertiser and Publishers' Circular. New York: J. & H. G. Langley, 1841–43.

Wilson, Halsey William. *The Bookman's Reading and Tools.* New York: H. W. Wilson Company, 1925.

Yankelovich, Skelly & White, Inc. *Consumer Research Study on Reading and Book Purchasing.* Darien, Conn.: Book Industry Study Group, 1978.

3. *Aftermarket*

Adams, Scott. *The O.P. Market: A Subject Directory to the Specialities of the Out-of-Print Book Trade.* New York: R. R. Bowker, 1943.

American Book Prices Current. New York: Bancroft-Parkman, 1895–.

Bacon, Edwin M. "Old Boston Booksellers." *The Bookman* 6 (February 1897): 542–46.

Barlow, William Pusey, Jr. *Book Collecting: Personal Rewards and Public Benefits; A Lecture Delivered at the Library of Congress on December 7, 1983.* Washington, D.C.: Library of Congress, 1984.

Basbanes, Nicholas A. *A Gentle Madness: Bibliophiles, Bibliomanes, and the Eternal Passion for Books.* New York: H. Holt, 1995.

Bookman's Price Index. Detroit: Gale Research, 1964–.

Briggs, Morris H. *Buying and Selling Rare Books.* New York: R. R. Bowker, 1927.

Bruno, Guido. *Adventures in American Bookshops, Antique Stores, and Auction Rooms.* Detroit: Douglas Book Shop, 1922.

Cannon, Carl L. *American Book Collectors and Collecting from Colonial Times to the Present.* New York: H. W. Wilson, 1941.

Carter, John. *ABC for Book Collectors.* Seventh edition. New Castle, Del.: Oak Knoll Press, 1997.

Caspar, C. N. *Directory of Antiquarian Booksellers and Dealers in Second-Hand Books of the United States.* Milwaukee: C. N. Caspar, 1885.

Dibdin, Thomas Frognall. *The Bibliomania; or, Book-Madness; Containing Some Account of the History, Symptoms, and Cure of This Fatal Disease, In an Epistle Addressed to Richard Hebers, Esq.* London: Longman, Hurst, Rees & Orme, 1809.

Heartman, Charles F., ed. *The American Book Collector.* Metuchen, N.J., 1932–35.

McKay, George L. *American Book Auction Catalogs, 1713–1934: A Union List.* New York: New York Public Library, 1937.

Meyers, Robin, and Michael Harris. *Antiquaries, Book Collectors, and the Circles of Learning.* Winchester: St. Paul's Bibliographies, 1996.

Pearson, David. *Provenance Research in Book History: A Handbook.* London: British Library, 1994.

Peters, Jean, ed. *Collectible Books: Some New Paths.* New York: R. R. Bowker, 1979.

Rostenberg, Leona, and Madeleine Stern. *Old Books, Rare Friends: Two Literary Sleuths and Their Shared Passion.* New York: Doubleday, 1997.

Stern, Madeleine. *Antiquarian Bookselling in the United States: A History from the Origins to the 1940s.* Westport, Conn.: Greenwood Press, 1985.

Stoddard, Roger E. *"Put a Resolute Hart to a Steep Hill": William Gowans, Antiquary and Bookseller: A Lecture. . . .* New York: Book Arts Press, School of Library Service, Columbia University, 1990.

United States Cumulative Book Auction Records. New York: Want List, The Book Trade Weekly, 1941–.

Wessen, Ernest J. *Rare Book Lore: Selections from the Letters of Ernest J. Wessen.* Edited by Jack Matthews. Athens: Ohio University Press, 1992.

Wilson, Robert A. *Modern Book Collecting.* New York: Knopf, 1980.

D. CONSUMERS

1. *Readers*

Addis, Patricia K., ed. *Through a Woman's I: An Annotated Bibliography of American Women's Autobiographical Writings, 1846–1976.* Metuchen, N.J.: Scarecrow Press, 1983.

Andrews, William L. *To Tell a Free Story: The First Century of Afro-American Autobiography, 1760–1865.* Urbana and Chicago: University of Illinois Press, 1986.

Arksey, Laura, Nancy Pries, and Marcia Reed, eds. *American Diaries: An Annotated Bibliography of Published American Diaries and Journals.* 2 vols. Detroit: Gale Research, 1983–87.

Benes, Peter, ed. *Early American Probate Inventories.* Boston: Boston University, 1989.

Brignano, Russell C. *Black Americans in Autobiography: An Annotated Bibliography of Autobiographies and Autobiographical Books Written since the Civil War.* Revised and expanded edition. Durham, N.C.: Duke University Press, 1984.

Briscoe, Mary Louise, and others. *American Autobiography, 1945–1980.* Madison: University of Wisconsin Press, 1982.

Brown, Richard D. *Knowledge Is Power: The Diffusion of Information in Early America, 1700–1865.* New York: Oxford University Press, 1989.

Bunkers, Suzanne L., and Cynthia A. Huff, eds. *Inscribing the Daily: Critical Essays on Women's Diaries.* Amherst: University of Massachusetts Press, 1996.

Butler, James Davie. *Commonplace Books; Why and How Kept: A Lecture; With Suggestions on Object and Method in Reading.* Hartford, Conn.: Barnard's American Journal of Education, 1887.

Butterfield, Stephen. *Black Autobiography in America.* Amherst: University of Massachusetts Press, 1974.

Cameron, Kenneth Walter. *Emerson and Thoreau as Readers: Selected Chapters from* The Transcendentalists and Minerva. Hartford: Transcendental Books, 1972.

————. *Ralph Waldo Emerson's Reading: A Guide for Source-Hunters and Scholars to the One Thousand Volumes Which He Withdrew from Libraries, Together with Some Unpublished Letters and a List of Emerson's Contemporaries, 1827–1850. . . .* New York: Haskell House, 1966.

Cantrell, Clyde Hull. "The Reading Habits of Ante-bellum Southerners." Ph.D. diss., University of Illinois, 1960.

Cornelius, Janet Duitsman. *When I Can Read My Title Clear: Literacy, Slavery, and Religion in the Antebellum South.* Columbia: University of South Carolina Press, 1991.

Crossley, Inc. *Continuing Study of Magazine Audiences.* Chicago: Time, Inc., 1946–47.

Cruse, Amy *The Victorians and Their Reading.* Boston: Houghton Mifflin, 1935.

Davidson, Cathy N., ed. *Reading in America: Literature and Social History.* Baltimore: Johns Hopkins University Press, 1989.

Davis, Charles T., and Henry Louis Gates Jr. *The Slave's Narrative.* Oxford: Oxford University Press, 1985.

Davis, Gwenn, and Beverly A. Joyce. *Personal Writings by Women to 1900: A Bibliography of American and British Writers.* Norman: University of Oklahoma Press, 1989.

Desmond, Jeanmarie. *Sundry Old Books: Reading Materials in Hampshire County Probate Inventories, 1760–1774.* Deerfield, Mass.: Historic Deerfield Summer Program, 1990.

Eakin, Paul John. *American Autobiography: Retrospect and Prospect.* Madison: University of Wisconsin Press, 1991.

Farren, Donald. "Subscription: A Study of the Eighteenth-Century American Book Trade." D.L.S. diss., Columbia University, 1982.

Fish, Stanley. *Is There a Text in This Class?: The Authority of Interpretive Communities.* Cambridge, Mass.: Harvard University Press, 1980.

————. "Literature in the Reader: Affective Stylistics." *New Literary History* 2 (1970): 123–62.

Frank, Stuart M., ed. and comp. *Meditations from Steerage: Two Whaling Journal Fragments. . . .* Sharon, Mass.: Kendall Whaling Museum, 1991.

Gallegos, Bernardo P. *Literacy, Education, and Society in New Mexico, 1693–1821.* Albuquerque: University of New Mexico Press, 1992.

Garvin, Harry R., ed. *Theories of Reading, Looking, and Listening.* Lewisburg, Pa.: Bucknell University Press, 1981.

Gernes, Todd S. "Check List of Albums and Commonplace Books at A.A.S." [Unpaged manuscript.] American Antiquarian Society, Worcester, Mass., 1991.

Gilmore, William J. "Elementary Literacy on the Eve of the Industrial Revolution: Trends in Rural New England, 1760–1830." *Proceedings of the American Antiquarian Society* 92, pt. 1 (April 1982): 87–178.

———. *Reading Becomes a Necessity of Life: Material and Cultural Life in Rural New England, 1780–1835.* Knoxville: University of Tennessee Press, 1989.

Goodfriend, Joyce D. *The Published Diaries and Letters of American Women: An Annotated Bibliography.* Boston: G. K. Hall, 1987.

Graff, Harvey J. *The Labyrinths of Literacy: Reflections on Literacy Past and Present.* London: Falmer Press, 1987.

———. *The Legacies of Literacy: Continuities and Contradictions in Western Culture and Society.* Bloomington and Indianapolis: Indiana University Press, 1987.

Gray, William Scott, and Ruth Monroe. *The Reading Interests and Habits of Adults: A Preliminary Report.* New York: Macmillan, 1929.

Gribben, Alan. "Private Libraries of American Authors: Dispersal, Custody, and Description." *Journal of Library History* 21 (1986): 300–314.

Hansen, Karen V., and Cameron L. Macdonald. "Research Note: Surveying the Dead Informant: Analysis and Historical Interpretation." *Qualitative Sociology* 18 (1995): 227–36.

Harding, Walter. *Emerson's Library.* Charlottesville: University Press of Virginia, 1967.

Harper & Brothers. *We Do Not Employ Agents; but the Following Are the Terms upon Which We Supply the Orders of Dealers, for Our Weekly Newspaper.* New York: Harper & Brothers, 1856.

Havlice, Patricia Pate. *And So to Bed: A Bibliography of Diaries Published in English.* Metuchen, N.J.: Scarecrow Press, 1987.

Hayes, Kevin J. *A Colonial Woman's Bookshelf.* Knoxville: University of Tennessee Press, 1996.

———. *The Library of William Byrd of Westover.* Madison, Wis.: Madison House, 1997.

Heininger, Mary Lynn Stevens. *At Home with a Book: Reading in America, 1840–1940*. Rochester, N.Y.: Strong Museum, 1986.

Henry Bill Publishing Co. *The Henry Bill Publishing Co.'s Private Instructions to Their Agents for Selling Their Subscription Books.* Norwich, Conn.: Henry Bill Publishing Co., 1874.

Hoffmann, Leonore, and Margo Culley. *Women's Personal Narratives: Essays in Criticism and Pedagogy.* New York: Modern Language Association of America, 1985.

Iser, Wolfgang. *The Implied Reader: Patterns of Communication in Prose Fiction from Bunyan to Beckett.* Baltimore: Johns Hopkins University Press, 1974.

Jackson, Leon. "The Reader Retailored: Thomas Carlyle, His American Audience, and the Politics of Evidence." *Book History* 2 (1999): 146–72.

Johnson, Clifton. *Old-Time Schools and School Books.* 1904; New York: P. Smith, 1935.

Jones Brothers & Co. *Agents' Companion: (Confidential) . . . By a Careful Daily Study of These All Important Practical Instructions, Your Work Becomes Easy and Your Success Sure.* Philadelphia and Cincinnati: Jones Brothers & Co., c. 1866–69.

Kaestle, Carl F. *Pillars of the Republic: Common Schools and American Society, 1780–1860.* New York: Hill & Wang, 1983.

Kaestle, Carl F., and others. *Literacy in the United States: Readers and Reading since 1880.* New Haven, Conn.: Yale University Press, 1991.

Kaplan, Louis, and others. *A Bibliography of American Autobiographies.* Madison: University of Wisconsin Press, 1961.

Keller-Cohen, Deborah, ed. *Literacy: Interdisciplinary Conversations.* Cresskill, N.J.: Hampton Press, 1994.

Kelley, Mary. "Reading Women/Women Reading: The Making of Learned Women in Antebellum America." *Journal of American History* 83 (1996): 401–24.

Kielbowicz, Richard B. *News in the Mail: The Press, Post Office, and Public Information, 1700–1860s.* New York: Greenwood Press, 1989.

Lee, Brian North. "Gentlemen and Their Book-Plates." In *Property of a Gentleman: The Formation, Organization and Dispersal of the Private Library, 1620–1920.* Edited by Robin Myers and Michael Harris. Winchester: St. Paul's Bibliographies, 1991.

Lehuu, Isabelle. "Changes in the Word: Reading Practices in Antebellum America." Ph.D. diss., Cornell University, 1992.

Leonard, Thomas C. "News at the Hearth: A Drama of Reading in Nineteenth-Century America." *Proceedings of the American Antiquarian Society* 102, pt. 2 (1993): 379–401.

————. *News for All: America's Coming-of-Age with the Press.* New York: Oxford University Press, 1995.

Link, Henry Charles, and Harry Arthur Hopf. *People and Books: A Study of Reading and Book-Buying Habits.* New York: Book Manufacturers' Institute, 1946.

Little, Elizabeth A. "Probate Records of Nantucket Indians." *Nantucket Algonquian Studies* 2 (1980): 1–72.

Lockridge, Kenneth A., ed. *The Diary, and Life, of William Byrd II of Virginia, 1674–1744.* Chapel Hill: University of North Carolina Press, 1987.

————. *Literacy in Colonial New England: An Enquiry into the Social Context of Literacy in the Early Modern West.* New York: W. W. Norton, 1974.

————. *On the Sources of Patriarchal Rage: The Commonplace Books of William Byrd and Thomas Jefferson and the Gendering of Power in the Eighteenth Century.* New York: New York University Press, 1992.

Machor, James L., ed. *Readers in History: Nineteenth-Century American Literature and the Contexts of Response.* Baltimore: Johns Hopkins University Press, 1993.

Mailloux, Steven. "Misreading as a Historical Act: Cultural Rhetoric, Bible Politics, and Fuller's 1845 Review of Douglass's *Narrative.*" In *Readers in History: Nineteenth-Century American Literature and the Contexts of Response.* Edited by James L. Machor. Baltimore: Johns Hopkins University Press, 1993.

Main, Gloria L. "Probate Records as a Source for Early American History." *William and Mary Quarterly* 32 (1975): 89–99.

Marcus, Jacob Rader. *Memoirs of American Jews 1775–1865.* 3 vols. Philadelphia: Jewish Publication Society of America, 1955.

Matthews, William, ed. *American Diaries: An Annotated Bibliography of American Diaries Written Prior to the Year 1861.* Berkeley and Los Angeles: University of California Press, 1945.

————. *American Diaries in Manuscript, 1580–1954: A Descriptive Bibliography.* Athens: University of Georgia Press, 1974.

McKinstry, E. Richard, ed. *Personal Accounts of Events, Travels, and Everyday Life in America: An Annotated Bibliography.* Winterthur, Del.: Henry Francis du Pont Winterthur Museum, 1997.

Monaghan, E. Jennifer. "Literacy Instruction and Gender in Colonial New England." In *Reading in America: Literature and Social History.* Edited by Cathy N. Davidson. Baltimore: Johns Hopkins University Press, 1989.

Moss, Ann. *Printed Commonplace-Books and the Structuring of Renaissance Thought.* Oxford: Clarendon Press, 1996.

Olsen, Mark, and Louis-Georges Harvey. "Reading in Revolutionary Times: Book Borrowing from the Harvard College Library, 1773–1782." *Harvard Library Bulletin* 4 (Fall 1993): 57–72.

Painter, Nell Irvin. "Representing Truth: Sojourner Truth's Knowing and Becoming Known." *Journal of American History* 81 (1994): 483–85.

Potter, Charles Francis. "Round Went the Album." *New York Folklore Quarterly* 4 (1948): 4–14.

Radway, Janice A. *Reading the Romance: Women, Patriarchy, and Popular Literature.* Chapel Hill: University of North Carolina Press, 1984.

Rawick, George, ed. *The American Slave: A Composite Autobiography.* 41 vols. Westport, Conn.: Greenwood Publishing, 1973–1980.

Reilly, Elizabeth Carroll. "Common and Learned Readers: Shared and Separate Spheres in Mid-Eighteenth-Century New England." 2 vols. Ph.D. diss., Boston University, 1994.

Resnick, Daniel P., ed. *Literacy in Historical Perspective.* Washington, D.C.: Library of Congress, 1983.

Robinson, F. J. G., and P. J. Wallis. *Book Subscription Lists: A Revised Guide.* Newcastle upon Tyne: Harold Hill, 1975.

Rose, Jonathan. "Rereading the English Common Reader: A Preface to the History of Audiences." *Journal of the History of Ideas* 53 (1992): 47–70.

Sealts, Merton M., Jr. *Melville's Reading.* Revised and enlarged edition. Columbia: University of South Carolina Press, 1988.

Sicherman, Barbara. "Reading and Ambition: M. Carey Thomas and Female Heroism." *American Quarterly* 45 (1993): 73–103.

Sinclair, Donald D., comp. *A Guide to Manuscript Diaries and Journals in the Special Collections Department, Rutgers University.* New Brunswick, N.J.: Rutgers University Library, 1980.

Smith, Roger H. *The American Reading Public: What It Reads, Why It Reads: From Inside Education and Publishing, View of Present Status, Future Trends. . . .* New York: R. R. Bowker, 1963.

Soltow, Lee, and Edward Stevens. *The Rise of Literacy and the Common School in the United States: A Socioeconomic Analysis to 1870.* Chicago: University of Chicago Press, 1981.

Stapp, Carol Buchalter. *Afro-Americans in Antebellum Boston: An Analysis of Probate Records.* 2 vols. New York: Garland, 1993.

Suleiman, Susan R., and Inge Crosman, eds. *The Reader in the Text: Essays on Audience and Interpretation.* Princeton, N.J.: Princeton University Press, 1980.

Tompkins, Jane P., ed. *Reader-Response Criticism: From Formalism to Post-Structuralism.* Baltimore: Johns Hopkins University Press, 1980.

Vail, R. W. G. [Seventeenth-Century American Book Labels.] *Publications of the American Antiquarian Society,* n.s. 42 (1932): 304–5; n.s. 43 (1933): 304–16.

Wallis, P. J. "Book Subscription Lists." *Library,* fifth ser. 29 (September 1974): 255–86.

———. *Publications in Historical Biobibliography.* Newcastle upon Tyne: University of Newcastle upon Tyne, Department of Education, January 1980.

Waples, Douglas. *Research Memorandum on Social Aspects of Reading in the Depression.* New York: Social Science Research Council, 1937.

Wilson, Douglas L., ed. *Jefferson's Literary Commonplace Book.* Princeton, N.J.: Princeton University Press, 1989.

Zboray, Ronald J. "Technology and the Character of Community Life in Antebellum America: The Role of Story Papers." In *Communication and Change in American Religious History.* Edited by Leonard I. Sweet. Grand Rapids, Mich.: William B. Eerdmans, 1993.

Zboray, Ronald J., and Mary Saracino Zboray. "Books, Reading, and the World of Goods in Antebellum New England." *American Quarterly* 48 (December 1996): 587–622.

———. "'Have You Read . . . ?': Real Readers and Their Responses in Antebellum Boston and Its Region." *Nineteenth-Century Literature* 52 (September 1997): 139–70.

———. "Political News and Female Readership in Antebellum Boston and Its Region." *Journalism History* 22 (Spring 1996): 2–14.

———. "Reading and Everyday Life in Antebellum Boston: The Diary of Daniel F. and Mary G. Child." *Libraries and Culture* 32 (July 1997): 285–323.

2. *Institutional Consumers*

American Sunday-School Union. *Catalogue of the Juvenile, Sunday-School, and Family Library. . . .* Philadelphia: American Sunday-School Union, 1845.

Annual Report of the Brattle Street Association for Aiding Religious Charities. Boston: Isaac R. Butts, 1826.

Annual Report of the New-York Unitarian Book Society. New York: Joseph C. Spear, Printer, 1823.

Augst, Thomas. "Making Society Out of Books: Character, Self-Fashioning, and the Rhetoric of Market Culture in Nineteenth-Century America." Ph.D. diss., Harvard University, 1996.

Bulletin of the American Library Association. Boston: American Library Association, 1907–38. Succeeded by *ALA Bulletin.* Chicago: American Library Association, 1939–69. Then, *American Libraries.* Chicago: American Library Association, 1970–.

Bulletin of the Public Library of the City of Boston. Boston: Boston Public Library, October 1867–January 1896.

Carpenter, Kenneth E. *Readers and Libraries: Toward a History of Libraries and Culture in America.* Washington, D.C.: Library of Congress, 1996.

Chartier, Roger. *The Order of Books: Readers, Authors, and Libraries in Europe between the Fourteenth and Eighteenth Centuries.* Translated by Lydia G. Cochrane. Stanford, Calif.: Stanford University Press, 1994.

Cole, John Y. *For Congress and Nation: A Chronological History of the Library of Congress.* Washington, D.C.: Library of Congress, 1979.

———. *Jefferson's Legacy: A Brief History of the Library of Congress.* Washington, D.C.: Library of Congress, 1993.

Dain, Phyllis. *The New York Public Library: A History of Its Founding and Early Years.* New York: New York Public Library, 1972.

Dain, Phyllis, and John Y. Cole, eds. *Libraries and Scholarly Communication in the United States: The Historical Dimension.* New York: Greenwood Press, 1990.

Davis, Donald G., Jr., and John Mark Tucker. *American Library History: A Comprehensive Guide to the Literature.* Santa Barbara, Calif.: ABC-CLIO, 1989.

Essex Circulating Library. *A Catalogue of the Essex Circulating Library, Kept by John M. Ives at His Book, Stationary [sic], and Music Store, Essex Street, Salem.* Salem, Mass.: John D. Cushing & Brothers, 1822.

Garrison, Dee. *Apostles of Culture: The Public Librarian and American Society, 1876–1920.* New York: Free Press, 1979.

Gross, Robert A. "Much Instruction from Little Reading: Books and Libraries in Thoreau's Concord." *Proceedings of the American Antiquarian Society* 97, pt. 1 (1987): 129–88.

Guild, Benjamin. *New Select Catalogue of Benjamin Guild's Circulating Library. . . .* Boston: printed for Benjamin Guild, 1789.

James Eastburn & Co. *Plan of Public Reading Rooms, on the Foundation of the Late E. Sargeants.* New York: private printing, 1812.

John S. Harvey & Son. *Circulating Library: Cheap Reading for the Long Evening!!* Broadside. Portsmouth, N.H.: private printing, 1854.

Karetsky, Stephen. *Reading Research and Librarianship: A Historical Analysis.* Westport, Conn.: Greenwood Press, 1982.

Larned, Josephus Nelson. *A Talk about Books: Addressed Originally to the Students of the Central High School, Buffalo.* Buffalo: Peter Paul Book, c. 1897.

The Library Bulletin. Boston: various publishers, 1869–72.

Library Company of Philadelphia. "Advertisement." In *Books Added to the Library since the Year 1741.* Philadelphia: Benjamin Franklin, 1746, 32.

"List of Books Composing the New Jersey School District Library." In *Annual Report of the Trustees of the School Fund of the State of New Jersey.* Trenton: Legislature of the State of New Jersey, 1840.

Mearns, David Chambers. *The Story up to Now: The Library of Congress, 1800–1946.* Washington, D.C.: U.S. Government Printing Office, 1947.

Potter, Alonzo. *Handbook for Readers and Students, Intended as a Help to Individuals, Associations, School-Districts, and Seminaries of Learning, in the Selection of Works for Reading, Investigation, or Professional Study.* New York: Harper & Brothers, 1843.

Rhees, William J. *Manual of Public Libraries, Institutions, and Societies, in the United States, and British Provinces of North America.* Philadelphia: J. B. Lippincott, 1859.

Rudolph, Frederick. *Curriculum: A History of the American Undergraduate Course of Study since 1636.* San Francisco: Jossey-Bass, 1977.

"The School Library." In *Third Annual Report of the Board of Education; Together with the Third Annual Report of the Secretary of the Board.* Boston: Marsh, Capen, Lyon & Webb, 1840, 12–17.

Shera, Jesse. *Foundations of the Public Library: The Origins of the Public Library Movement in New England, 1692–1855.* Chicago: University of Chicago Press, 1949.

Taylor, Archer. *Book Catalogues: Their Varieties and Uses.* Second edition. New York: F. C. Beil, 1986.

Willison, Ian R. *On the History of Libraries and Scholarship: A Paper Presented before the Library History Round Table of the American Library Association, June 26, 1979.* Washington, D.C.: Library of Congress, 1980.

Wilson, Louis R. *The Geography of Reading: A Study of the Distribution and Status of Libraries in the United States.* Chicago: American Library Association and University of Chicago Press, 1938.

Winans, Robert B. *A Descriptive Checklist of Book Catalogues Separately Printed in America, 1693–1800.* Worcester, Mass.: American Antiquarian Society, 1981.

———. "The Reading of English Novels in Eighteenth-Century America, 1750–1800." Ph.D. diss., New York University, 1972.

Zboray, Ronald J. "Reading Patterns in Antebellum America: Evidence in the Charge Records of the New York Society Library." *Libraries and Culture* 26 (1991): 301–33.

3. *The Book Trade Itself*

Baym, Nina. *Novels, Readers, and Reviewers: Responses to Fiction in Antebellum America.* Ithaca, N.Y.: Cornell University Press, 1984.

Brodowski, Joyce Helene. "Literary Piracy in England from the Restoration to the Early Eighteenth Century." Ph.D. diss., Columbia University, 1973.

Feather, John. *Publishing, Piracy and Politics: An Historical Study of Copyright in Britain.* New York: Mansell, 1994.

Graffagnino, J. Kevin, comp. *Only in Books: Writers, Readers and Bibliophiles on Their Passion.* Madison, Wis.: Madison House, 1996.

Judge, Cyril Bathurst. *Elizabethan Book-Pirates.* Cambridge, Mass.: Harvard University Press, 1934.

LaFollette, Marcel C. *Stealing into Print: Fraud, Plagiarism, and Misconduct in Scientific Publishing.* Berkeley: University of California Press, 1992.

Pritchard, John Paul. *The Literary Wise Men of Gotham: Criticism in New York, 1815–1860.* Baton Rouge: Louisiana State University Press, 1963.

Rubin, Joan Shelley. *The Making of Middle-Brow Culture.* Chapel Hill: University of North Carolina Press, 1992.

Sielke, Sabine. *Fashioning the Female Subject: The Intertextual Networking of Dickinson, Moore, and Rich.* Ann Arbor: University of Michigan Press, 1997.

III. CONCLUSION: THE FUTURE OF BOOK HISTORY

Barzun, Jacques. *The Bibliophile of the Future, His Complaints about the Twentieth Century: Delivered on the Occasion of the Fourth Annual Bromsen Lecture, May 1, 1976.* Boston: Trustees of the Boston Public Library, 1976.

Bloch, R. Howard, and Carla Hesse. *Future Libraries.* Berkeley: University of California Press, 1993.

Cole, John Y., ed. *Books in Our Future: Perspectives and Proposals.* Washington, D.C.: Library of Congress, 1987.

Index

Ronald J. Zboray is associate professor of history at Georgia State University, and Mary Saracino Zboray is a research associate at the same institution. Together they have published extensively on antebellum cultural history, including recent articles in journals such as *American Quarterly, American Studies, Journal of the Early Republic, Journalism History, Libraries & Culture, Nineteenth-Century Contexts,* and *Nineteenth-Century Literature,* and essays in two collections, on Boston business history and on Transcendentalism, published by the Massachusetts Historical Society. After receiving his Ph.D. in American civilization from New York University in 1984, Ronald Zboray co-edited *The Emma Goldman Papers: A Microfilm Edition* (Alexandria, Va.: Chadwyck-Healey, 1990) and authored *A Fictive People: Antebellum Economic Development and the American Reading Public* (New York: Oxford University Press, 1993). Mary Zboray received her M.A. in anthropology from the graduate faculty of the New School for Social Research in 1980, and did doctoral work at George Washington University in American studies, where she was the 1982–83 Smithsonian Fellow.

During 1998–99, the Zborays were Honorary Visiting Fellows at the Schlesinger Library, Radcliffe College, while completing their book on the experience of reading in antebellum New England. For this purpose, Ronald Zboray received a Fellowship for University Teachers from the National Endowment for the Humanities, which was matched by Georgia State University. In 1997 the Zborays won the Cathy Covert Prize in Mass Communication from the Association for Education in Journalism and Mass Communication for their article "Political News and Female Readership in Antebellum Boston and Its Region," which appeared in *Journalism History* (1996).

155

Book design by Christopher Kuntze

Printed and bound by Thomson-Shore